All the best

Ralph

Creating the Outstanding School

Creating the Outstanding School

David Lynch

Jake Madden

Tina Doe

with

Richard Smith, Steve Provost and Helen Spiers

National Library of Australia Cataloguing-in-Publication entry

Title: Creating the outstanding school
Author: David Lynch, Jake Madden, Tina Doe
Co-Author: Richard Smith, Steve Provost, Helen Spiers.
ISBN: 9781329385436 (paperback)
Subjects: Educational leadership--Australia.
Mentoring in education--Australia.
Effective teaching--Australia.
Educational innovations--Australia.

Dewey Number: 371.2011

**First Published in 2015
by Oxford Global Press
London (UK)**
www.oxfordglobalpress.com

Every effort has been made to trace and acknowledge copyright. However should any infringement have occurred, the publisher and the author tenders their apology and invite the copyright owner to contact them so the infringement may be remedied.

 These works have been peer reviewed.

Contents

About the Authors

Professor David Lynch

David Lynch is Professor of Education in the School of Education at Southern Cross University. He is the author of numerous articles and texts on teacher education and related matters and one of Australia's foremost teacher education innovators. His research and development interests form the basis of a radical rethink on teaching and teacher education and these are reflected in his seminal published works over the past fifteen years. He has had a distinguished academic career at several universities in Australia, having held a number of senior academic leadership positions, and consults in education jurisdictions across the globe.

Dr Jake Madden

Jake Madden has served as a principal of five schools and is currently the principal of Dar Al Marefa Private School, Dubai, UAE. He is passionate about leadership and the positive difference that it can make to teacher and student learning outcomes. Over many years, Jake has led and facilitated the professional learning of principals and staff at school and national and international level in the area of leadership, school improvement and curriculum development. His educational interests lie in building teacher capacity. He is widely published in this area of teachers as researchers, authoring two books and a number of journal articles showcasing his experiences and research into leading educational change. He is currently an Adjunct with Southern Cross University and is on the editorial board for the International Journal of Innovation, Creativity and Change.

Dr Tina Doe

Tina Doe is an Education Consultant who leads the design of 'purpose-fit' Teacher Professional Learning Initiatives (TPLI) that focus community networks to pedagogical practice. Her Instructional Leadership Model (the TPLI) underpins her signature Professional Learning Clinic: *High impact Instructional Leadership which* won the inaugural 2015 Jack Pizzey Leadership Team prize for Qld State Education. The expertise she brings to the demonstration of high yield practices through common pedagogical language is significant in its enhancement/generation of professional learning communities through feedback, coaching and reflection. Tina has been a senior executive in schools and universities and is currently Editor of the International Journal of Innovation, Creativity and Change.

Emeritus Professor Richard Smith

Richard Smith is an Adjunct Professor of Education at Southern Cross University. In his career he has been President of the *Australian Association for Research in Education* (AARE), editor of the *Australian Journal of Education* and chair of the Queensland Minister for Education's *Ministerial Advisory Committee for Educational Renewal*. He is presently chair of the Board of Directors at the Australian Institute of Music, a ministerial nominee on the *Flexible Literacy for Remote Primary Schools Programme Advisory Committee*, a director of the *Good to Great Schools Australia* Board and a member of the *Australian Institute of Company Directors*. Richard has held positions ranging from lecturer to Executive Dean of Schools of Education where he developed innovative approaches to teacher education and published widely in the teacher education field. He established the pioneering *Bachelor of Learning Management* (BLM) in 2000 and, with David Lynch, has advocated a greater emphasis on evidence-based pedagogical strategies in teacher education tied to improved student outcomes.

Dr Steven Provost

Steve Provost teaches experimental psychology, behaviour analysis and methodology in the School of Health and Human Sciences at Southern Cross University. He has published work in learning, human factors and psychopharmacology. More recently, the focus of his research interests has been in teaching and learning in higher education. He received the Australian Psychological Society's Award for Distinguished Contribution to Psychology Education in 2010. He was a member of the team of authors responsible for the publication of an Australian and NZ edition of Doug Bernstein's introductory text "Psychology: An International Discipline in Context".

Dr Helen Spiers

Helen Spiers is currently the Principal of Kormilda College, a T-12 Independent International Baccalaureate school in Darwin, Northern Territory, Australia. Helen commenced at Kormilda College in July 2007 as Deputy Principal and brought with her more than 20 years' experience as an educator in the Northern Territory and South Australia, across secondary and tertiary education. Helen previously spent 13 years managing VET programs across the Jabiru-Western Arnhelmand region before joining the Charles Darwin University as a Mathematics educator. During this time, she completed several post-graduate qualifications and recently added the AICD Company Directors Course to her professional portfolio. In 2010 Helen completed her Doctorate with research entitled *'Indigenous participation in tertiary education: elements of the institutional learning environment critical for course completion'* and is currently establishing an active research hub at Kormilda College in affiliation with the School of Education at the Charles Darwin University, Southern Cross University, New South Wales and Edith Cowan University, Western Australia. Her research interests lie within the areas of Indigenous Education and Teacher Effectiveness.

1. Creating the Outstanding School

David Lynch, Jake Madden and Tina Doe

In this book we provide an insight into what it means to create the outstanding school. Our aim in writing this book is to stimulate thought and to provide some guidance into what, for many, is now a many decades long school reform aspiration. The book does not purport to be conclusive in its scope towards such an aspiration, but it does seek to signal and then explain key elements which, from our own research work in schools and in teacher education over the past twenty or so years, and that of other noted researchers, lie at the heart of creating the outstanding school. In effect we bring to bear what we have discovered after conducting pioneering research focused on 'teaching', 'teacher learning', 'the leadership of teaching' and the organization of schools.

In working towards such an agenda we feature the *Collaborative Teacher Learning Model* (See Chapters 2 and 5) and its key elements of 'teaching,' 'leadership', 'team teaching', 'coaching', 'mentoring', 'feedback', 'data driven decision making' 'high impact instruction' and the idea of 'teachers as researchers' as the embodiment of a school-based strategy for creating the outstanding school. Each chapter explores associated concepts in greater detail and the book, when read in its entirety, comes to represent an insight into what 'creating the outstanding school' means and thus requires.

But as the book will reveal, this 'outstanding school' agenda is complex and enmeshed in socio-economic change, not to mention various political agendas, that is redefining what it means to work and live in the 2000's. With this point in mind, we commence this introductory chapter with an elaboration of such an environment to highlight key points for later reference.

Education, Change and Government Policy

Education is now front and centre in the minds of governments across the globe. National and international student performance benchmarks, such as PISA[1] and ISA[2] are commonplace and being used to judge the performance of schooling systems. These testing regimes have created a global competition in education, such that Governments strive to enact policies in an attempt to ensure that their education systems exceed the performance of their trading partners and of course that these systems contribute to the standard of living of their citizens. The important point is the key role that education now plays in positioning economies for high-value trade and high standards of living[3] (Australian Government, 2009; OECD, 2011; 1996).

This era can be explained by the emergence of the Knowledge Economy (OECD, 1996). The Knowledge Economy can be defined as an economy built on the wealth created from *'know-how'*. That is, the selling of technology based products for cash, exchanging them for something else of value or leveraging them to create added value. In comparison, the former 'industrial economy' relies predominantly on the sale of raw resources, commodities and primary processing to generate income and wealth: a stratified and well-organised chain of 'human labour' is a key requirement (Smith and Lynch, 2010; Powell and Snellman, 2004).

In contrast to this industrial economy, the key commodity in the Knowledge Economy is *knowledge* and its use in new and interconnected ways to create what appears a voracious and endless cycle of new products and services coming to market and which are

---

[1] See http://www.oecd.org/pisa/
[2] See http://www.acer.edu.au/isa
[3] See http://www.oecdbetterlifeindex.org/countries/australia/

available to a world-wide set of consumers. This new circumstance requires a confluence of 'human brain power' networks, each working simultaneously towards a product or service. The workforce required is thus highly educated within all sections and across all levels of the economy (Powell and Snellman, 2004; Doyle, Kurth & Kerre, 2000; Donkin, 1998). This circumstance implicates education systems and their schools for an appropriate and sustainable response (Lynch, 2012). Chapters in this book provide an insight into what such a response might involve. At the heart of each chapter is a goal to seed the creation of the outstanding school.

Having made these introductory statements our task now is to explore what is meant by the term 'outstanding school' and then provide a preliminary insight into what is required for it to be achieved. We conclude the chapter by outlining each subsequent chapter.

Towards the Outstanding School

A 'Google' search for *what is an outstanding school?* reveals a plethora of websites, articles, reports, publications and the like, each arguing a perspective on education. At the heart of each however is an implicit understanding that it is desirable and importantly that it embodies a set of 'things' (articulated as learning goals) which are achieved in **every** student at specifically defined 'schooling' junctures. The emphasis upon 'every' student is important here because the Knowledge Economy --- putting aside the social justice issue in not achieving this --- has few places for the low or unskilled: to such an extent that the jobs that do become available for such people are often menial, short term and low paid and of course not fully contributing to the premise of the Knowledge Economy. On a social outcomes front, mortality and imprisonment rates rise markedly as educational attainment decreases (OECD, 2011).

Further, social cohesion is informed by education. Education also enables networks to form that have "shared norms, values and understanding that facilitate co-operation within or among groups" and which creates the environment for innovations and advancements which in turn add to the quality of life of a country (OECD 2001 cited in Dijkstra and de la Motte, 2014, p.8).

While we could delve deeper into this circumstance given the diversity of nation states and how the Knowledge Economy is playing out in each, our task in writing this book is best served by stating categorically that schooling and teaching are now fundamentals in this new society circumstance. But we emphasize that inherent schooling and teaching tasks are complex, enmeshed in numerous 'modern day' socio-cultural considerations (i.e. changing faces of 'the family'; children in long day care, less adherence to traditional mainstays such as 'The Church', people more informed and more likely to question supposed 'truths', to name but a few) and subject to constant changes (Lynch, 2012).

To highlight this 'complexity', schools, in addition to 'delivering' the State curriculum, are increasingly being called upon to remedy emerging social ills, in a belief by governments that schools are best placed to deal with such matters (meaning convenient and already mobilized into each local community). Issues such as; drug and alcohol awareness, personal safety, as well as diverse agendas ranging from 'surf safety' to 'career counseling' to 'moral upbringing' and civics[4], further complicate what has now become an over-crowded curriculum for schools. This is perhaps a case of modern society failing to keep pace with an unprecedented rate of new and emergent issues (Griffin, et al, 2012). In any case the 'outstanding school' has to deal with such a circumstance and likewise achieve in it (Lynch, 2012).

---

[4] See for example
http://education.qld.gov.au/curriculum/jointventure/govt/ddemo/choosing/formal.html#informal

While it can be argued that schools have always played such a key role, the difference today is that the stakes in education failure has just got higher and the consequences more dire for the individual student.

In simple terms modern society requires each of its citizens to have a sound education. Failure at school is not an option and so it is incumbent on the School to 'design' so **each** student achieves prescribed learning outcomes at key learning junctures. This is a tall order, but it does get to the heart of what the outstanding school comes to mean. We can thus have a go at defining the outstanding school as one which *has the sustained capacity to achieve defined sets of learning outcomes, in _every_ student, at key schooling junctures.*

So What Contributes to the Outstanding School?

As previous sections indicated the work context for schools and their teachers is complex, fast changing with various entanglements: at face value reforming a school so *every student achieves* appears a daunting task. But understanding where 'impact' is best rendered is a key first step. We are assisted in this understanding by John Hattie (2009, 2011, 2012) who conducted a synthesis of over 800 meta-analyses relating to student achievement. He identified five variables which have the capacity to impact student achievement. These are:

- The Student
- The Student's Home Life
- The School
- The Curriculum
- Approaches to Teaching

Hattie's (2009) central finding however is that 'what teachers do matters'.

In terms of 'the student', Hattie (2009) argues it's what the child brings to school that influences their achievement (from preschool, home, and genetics) as well as a set of personal dispositions that can have marked effect on the outcomes of their schooling. 'The home' can either nurture and support achievement of students, or it can be harmful and destructive. In terms of the 'other' Hattie (2009) variables: 'the school', 'its curriculum' and the 'approach to teaching', Hattie has thus identified for teachers and schools three strategic remediation or 'strategic focus' areas that directly contribute to creating the outstanding school. While 'the student' and 'the home' are not in the realm of the school to remedy pragmatically, 'the school', 'the curriculum' and the 'approaches to teaching' are well within scope. In fact these three areas come to represent what a school needs to attend to if it is to path itself to becoming the 'outstanding school'. We focus on these three elements by outlining key processes and strategies in chapters, which follow.

Returning to the theme of 'Creating the Outstanding School', we must also appreciate that the research literature indicates that "the quality of an education system cannot exceed the quality of its teachers" (Barber and Mourshed 2007, p.13). Putting this finding with those of Hattie (2009, 2011, 2012) and the message becomes one focused on a need to improve the teaching capacities of **all the school's teachers**. To sharpen this statement further we've identified a series of key findings from the education research literature. Each, while not comprehensively representing what is in the literature on such a topic, does come to represent key insights into what constitutes 'strategy' when creating the outstanding school. They also formulate for the reader a set of further readings to better understand the premise of this book[5]. They also front end discussions in sequent chapters. These key findings are:

1. A Focus on Teacher Professional Learning

- To improve student learning, professional learning needs to be conceived both as a means for improving

---

[5] We are assisted in this process by references to
http://www.education.vic.gov.au/Documents/about/department/teachingprofession.pdf

teacher effectiveness and as a means for improving the effectiveness of schools. (Cole, 2012, p.6)

- Effective professional learning focuses on developing the core attributes of an effective teacher. (Cole, 2012, p.6)

- Improvement is a discipline, a practice that requires focus, knowledge, persistence and consistency over time. (Elmore, 2008, p.13)

- Targeted professional learning should 'become part of the expectations for teachers' roles and form an integral part of the culture of a school'. (Lieberman 1995, p. 593)

2. Teachers working together on improving their teaching

- ...collaborative cultures build social capital and therefore also professional capital in a school's community. They accumulate and circulate knowledge and ideas, as well as assistance and support that help teachers become more effective, increase their confidence, and encourage them to be more open to and actively engaged in change. (Hargreaves and Fullan, 2012, p.114)

- Schools that function as professional communities are four times more likely to be improving academically. (Lewis, 2002, p.488)

- Teachers learn from each other and share good teaching practices through a range of opportunities at school and system levels. Observing and giving feedback on each other's practice is the norm. (From New Directions to Action 2013, p. 13[6])

---

[6] http://www.education.vic.gov.au/Documents/about/department/teachingprofession.pdf

- "The focus must shift from helping individuals become more effective in their isolated classrooms and schools, to creating a new collaborative culture based on interdependence, shared responsibility, and mutual accountability". (Dufour and Marzano 2011, p.67)

3. A Focus on Instruction

- ...you cannot change learning and performance at scale without creating a strong, visible, transparent culture of instructional practice. (City, Elmore et al. 2009, p.32)
- [Educators] must be hungry for evidence of student learning and use that evidence to drive continuous improvement...(Dufour and Marzano 2011, p.24)
- Effective systems have developed an integrated set of measures that show what teachers do and what happens as a result. (Darling-Hammond et al., 2011, p.10)
- The only way we can accomplish the changes we need is through intense focus in improving classroom practice. We can do it by declaring that this is the focus: reduce bad variation by increasing consistency. Teachers and teacher leaders will have to take a risk here. It is the one area that is within the control of teachers – break down the autonomy of the classroom so that greater consistency of practice can be achieved. (Fullan, 2006, p.58)
- If we want students to learn more, teachers must become students of their own teaching. (Kane, 2013)

4. Feedback on Teaching Performance

- The majority of Australian teachers reported that evaluation of their work is largely done simply to fulfil administrative requirements and that their work has little impact on the way they teach in the classroom. (OECD, 2009)

- Performers can only adjust their performance successfully if the information fed back to them is stable, accurate, and trustworthy. (Wiggins, 2012, p.13)

- Meaningful appraisal is geared to teacher development and improvements in learning. It helps teachers improve their teaching skills by identifying and developing specific aspects of their teaching. It improves the way they relate to students and colleagues and their job satisfaction, and has a large impact on student outcomes. (Jensen, 2011, p.7)

The implication of these four elements is that school leaders must first know how well each teacher is performing and then devise an improvement strategy to positively impact the teaching performance of each teacher. To this end, subsequent chapters focus on an aspect of these four elements as a cohesive teaching improvement strategy

Let's now recap where we are at in terms of our discussions thus far.

We've established that the outstanding school is one that enables each and every student to sustainably achieve *all* the predefined learning outcomes at key schooling junctures. In many ways this is about ensuring 'no kid gets left behind'! These outcomes come to represent the ambitions of society and are reflective of prevailing education policies globally. As Hattie (2009) indicates it is the work of the teacher that matters in such equations and thus any moves towards creating the outstanding school must have a focus on the 'teacher and their teaching capacities'. While the teacher's teaching is central in focus, strategies that positively influence 'the child' and 'their home' and which mobilise 'the curriculum' and 'the school' for teaching effect are further 'foundation' considerations in this quest.

Having made these introductory comments we now prefigure chapters in this book.

Prefiguring this Book

Each chapter in this book informs an aspect of 'Creating the Outstanding School'. To organise the book and to do justice to the chapters included, we briefly introduce each one.

Chapter 2 case studies a school which undertook a five year 'create the outstanding school' journey. In general terms, the school consolidated current knowledge about effective teaching and learning into a cohesive, whole of school approach for teaching improvement. This school in effect tested propositions that lie at the heart of this book. This strategy is termed the *Collaborative Teacher Learning Model* (CTLM) and is based on an approach to school leadership, where a coaching, mentoring and feedback regime for classroom teachers is coupled to 'research and data' to improve student outcomes. The chapter concludes with a presentation of research data associated with this strategy. In presenting this chapter early in the book we seek to illustrate the fundamentals of the 'creating the outstanding school journey' and to prefigure key elements, which are then expanded on in subsequent chapters. Chapter 2 in effect stands to illustrate what is possible when key knowledge in this book is brought to bear on a school for student learning gain.

Central to the Collaborative Teacher Learning Model in Chapter 2 is the notion of 'using data' to inform teaching decision-making. *Chapter 3* provides an outline of how school leaders can use teaching and learning data to improve their overall school teaching performance.

Chapter 4 introduces the concepts of coaching, mentoring and feedback by providing a comprehensive review of the literature as it relates to each in an education context. This foundations *Chapter 5*, where the 'how to implement' a coaching, mentoring and feedback regime is explained. The central premise of the chapter is an understanding that it requires for effect an orchestration of 'leadership' and 'data driven decision making', which are then consolidated into a 'coaching, mentoring and feedback' regime at the classroom teacher level. To explain the 'how to' we revisit the Collaborative Teacher Learning Model and use it to scaffold an insight into the key elements required for implementation.

In *Chapter 6* the Teacher Professional Learning Initiative (TPLI) is presented as an approach to teacher professional learning. The TPLI has been conceptualised as a 'purpose-fit' teaching enhancement model and is specifically designed to maximize the benefits of a teacher professional development program.

To this point in the book outlined chapters have focused on teaching improvement models and a set of related understandings that create the environment and mechanisms through which the outstanding school is created. Book chapters now transition their focus to the embodiments of the outstanding school.

In *Chapter 7* we examine the premise of the 'required' learning environment. The central tenant of the chapter is that there is growing research evidence that a well designed and orchestrated learning environment contributes to the improvement of teaching practices and to student learning.

Chapter 8 examines the premise of planning the outstanding lesson. In discussing such fundamentals we make the point that the outstanding school is commensurate to outstanding lessons. To this end we take the reader back, as it were, to initial teacher education and focus on a process that scaffolds the design of the 'outstanding lesson'. On another plane, this chapter also creates a set of underlying considerations, which in turn inform 'the what' that one coaches, mentors and provides feedback to teachers on.

Chapter 9 examines what is meant and thus required for the creation of a teaching performance culture in a school. Key to the chapter is the notion of 'teaching feedback'. The chapter examines the concept of feedback in greater detail and concludes by providing a model for its implementation.

Chapter 10 examines the concept of teachers as researchers. The 'teacher as researcher' concept comes to represent a strategy for enabling teachers to better understand their profession, to make informed teaching decisions and to contribute to the growth of their profession by making valid contributions to it. Not to mention a new way for teachers to approach and engage with teacher professional learning. Taken together, the teacher as researcher concept can perhaps be described as a Knowledge Economy strategy for teacher professional learning, where teachers collect and interpret data for teaching and learning effect.

Chapter 11 concludes the book by providing an insight into the *Collaborative Teacher Learning Model* and how it is being implemented in a school with many inherent challenges. In effect the chapter case studies how one school is building on findings, as outlined in this book, for direct school-wide improvement.

Having now made these introductory comments about the book and each chapter we now invite you to begin the journey into understanding the creation of the outstanding school.

2. A Study into Creating the Outstanding School

David Lynch, Richard Smith, Jake Madden and Steve Provost

This chapter outlines a study into a school reform strategy that consolidated current knowledge about effective teaching and learning into a cohesive, whole of school approach for teaching improvement. This strategy is termed the Collaborative Teacher Learning Model or CTLM. This strategy is based on an approach to school leadership, where a coaching, mentoring and feedback regime for classroom teachers is used to improve student outcomes in the curriculum area of English. The chapter concludes with a presentation of data associated with this strategy.

Introduction

Across the globe governments have begun to focus their education policies to improving their education system outcomes. International comparative studies of student achievement, such as the *Programme for International Student Assessment* [PISA], have been used as the performance reference (see OECD, 2013; 2010a; 2010b). This focus is such that "a global competition in educational achievement in core subject matter areas like reading, arithmetic/mathematics and science" has emerged (Scheerens, 2013, p.16). This enthusiasm, as we outlined in Chapter 1 stems from the highly competitive trade environment that a knowledge-based economy (OECD, 1996) has intensified since the 1990s. More pointedly numerous reports over past decades cite the economic benefits of maintaining high performing education systems in such a global knowledge-based economy (see for example, Hanushek, and Woessmann, 2009, 2010; MCEETYA, 2008; Access Economic, 2005; Barro, 2001).

On a related plane, education researchers such as Hattie (2012, 2011, 2009) and Hargreaves and Fullan (2012), having released studies which specifically implicate the teaching capacities of individual teachers in such student performance results, have further intensified government preoccupation with improving their respective schooling system's performance. This preoccupation has "created global policy convergence toward high-stakes testing in schools and the use of test results to 'steer at a distance', particularly as it applies to policy-makers' promise to improve teacher quality" (Thompson and Cook, 2014, p.16). Taking into account what schools and education systems can readily control and deal with, a focus on teachers and their teaching has become key in associated school reforms. Or, as Hattie (2008) suggests, it is what teachers know, do, and care about which is very powerful in this learning equation. It therefore follows that a pathway to success, in terms of enhanced learning outcomes in students, is what will enable teachers to become better teachers (Hargreaves & Fullan, 2012; Hattie, 2009) and together an outstanding school.

The challenge for schools in all this and chiefly for the Head, who is charged with effecting such policy positions, is to implement a strategy that sustainably improves the teaching capacities of all their teachers.

In this chapter we provide an insight into one such strategy: a strategy that brings to bear current knowledge about effective teaching and learning into a cohesive whole of school strategy for teaching improvement. This strategy is termed the *Collaborative Teacher Learning Model* or CTLM (see Table 1 at chapter's end for an overview of the theoretical and conceptual elements). In brief, this strategy is based on an approach to school leadership, where a coaching, mentoring and feedback regime for classroom teachers is used to improve student outcomes, and in the context of this case study, in the curriculum area of English (a component of the Australian K-10 English curriculum). The curriculum area of English was used to focus the strategy into the school as it was perceived by the Head as being singularly important, as it underpinned the academic skills for all other curriculum areas (Madden, 2012). A presentation, in a later section, of preliminary data associated with this strategy provides an insight into the strategy's efficacy. The CTLM and its key elements are explored in greater detail in later chapters.

We turn first to an outlining of the concepts of alignment, capability and engagement as background theory information for the overall school strategy and for later reference purposes.

Alignment, Capability and Engagement

Programs such as PISA have had the effect of encouraging a greater interest and concern with the concepts of 'educational effectiveness' and 'school improvement' although the distinction between them has eroded (Creemers and Kyriakides, 2012). As Scheerens (2013, pp. 5-6) observes, effectiveness refers to "causality between means and ends in a complex practical situation, and therefore is analytically difficult". Moreover, this very characteristic of concern for 'causes' of intended effects is of great practical relevance because of its potential for school improvement.

Scheerens (2013, p. 6) goes on to identify the main threads in school improvement research, namely equality of opportunities in education and the significance of the school; economic studies on education production functions; evaluation of compensatory programs and school improvement programs; studies of unusually effective schools; studies of the effectiveness of teachers, classes and instructional procedures and studies of the effectiveness of system level policies and institutional arrangements.

Schiemann's (2014, p. 282) work provides an alternative way of approaching institutional behaviour and effectiveness by "focussing on 'talent', or the collective knowledge, skills, abilities, experiences, values, habits and behaviours of all labour that is brought to bear on the organisation's mission". He proposes that 'talent management' is a process of dealing with resources to reach benefits beyond financial ones alone.

People are conceptualised as 'embedded' in the organisation rather than as being 'employed'. This approach has compelling characteristics to it in so far as it links the recruitment, training, retention, satisfaction and effectiveness of staff with organisational visions and goals and integrates the activities and responsibilities of the 'talent life cycle' regardless of geography and the kind of organisation. The talent life cycle according to Schiemann is the terrain on which most people engage with the organisation and reflects the organisational investment in its activities. In this way, there are mutual obligations between the organisation and embedded people. Optimising talent in the full talent life cycle is a complex process that determines the effectiveness of talent investments (Schiemann, 2014, p. 282). Managers and coaches within the organisation are the people ideally situated to optimise people investments. "Great leaders", Ralph Izzo, CEO of Public Service Enterprise[7] suggests, "know how to optimise their talent by focusing it, developing the right capabilities, and creating engagement" (Cited in Schiemann, 2013, p. 283). Thus,

> "If a leader doesn't have people who are aligned with the goals and vision, have effective competencies and are engaged in the task at hand, isn't something wrong? Is that leader the right person for a job that requires talent optimization?" (Schiemann, 2013, p. 283).

---

[7] https://www.pseg.com/family/leadership/ceo.jsp

Schiemann (2014, p. 283) proposes a model entitled 'People Equity' which conceptualises the effective management of human talent regardless of industry or global location" and which has proved to be a helpful framework for coordinating the entire talent lifecycle (Schiemann, 2009, 2012). The core categories of the model are *Alignment, Capabilities and Engagement* or ACE. These distinctive but interdependent categories include synchrony of people with the goals, clientele and brand of the organisation, wherever they are located within it. Again, capabilities are defined as the available knowledge, skill, information and resources available to people sufficient to meet the organisation's goals. Last, engagement includes people satisfaction, commitment and willingness to take action for the benefit of the organisation in a discretionary way. Together these categories provide an agenda for understanding and exploring the main issues in the school effectiveness literature.

That is, the ACE model offers a potential mechanism for identifying and measuring 'genuine school effects' by showing the magnitude of the effect from one school compared to the next. Further, the degree of this effect can be explained by "malleable conditions defined at the school level" (Scheerens, 2013, p. 8). To reach such outcomes, it is strategically important to know if talent investments have been optimized. School Heads need to be capable of recognising the importance of the talent life cycle and implementing the appropriate procedures.

Having located the theory of talent management we now progress with an explanation of the School's teaching improvement strategy (or CTLM) using the elements of Alignment, Capabilities and Engagement as organisers.

A Teaching Improvement Strategy: *The CTLM*

In developing the Collaborative Teacher Learning Model (CTLM), the Head reported a plethora of available school change literature, each presenting a position for improving the performance of the school. This surfeit, coupled with the 'day-to-day' demands of Headship created the initial challenge for him in deciding where and when to start and what to focus on for optimal effect (Ferrandino, 2014; City, 2013; Sogunro, 2012). His concern was captured by questions such as: what is critical in the literature and how might these critical elements be arranged and in what order for teaching effect and what measures are needed to inform and ascertain teaching effect? In coming to terms with such challenges he enlisted the help of the local University[8] to distil the literature into plan form. What resulted was the CTLM, which comprises five inter-related elements, which have been arranged and then sustained within the school for teaching effect. Figure 1 provides an overview of the CTLM and how each element relates to one and other, while Table 1 (at the chapter's end) provides specific details for each element and the literature, which informs same.

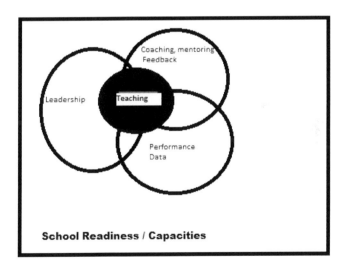

Figure 1: Collaborative Teacher Learning Model

---

[8] Southern Cross University, Australia. www.scu.edu.au

At the outset, it is important to point out that the central feature of the CTLM is an evidence based practice scheme (i.e. the school collected and referenced their decisions to various performance data as well as embedding their decision making in evidence based literature) coupled to a teaching team-based coaching, mentoring and feedback regime. This coupling provides the central mechanism through which the teaching performance of each teacher is assessed and where the strategy for improvement is planned and enacted. This mechanism is informed by a school-wide data collection and management system where timely reports on student progress, using standardised testing results[9] and effect size calculations (we elaborate this concept in a later section) are provided to each teaching team.

The leadership of the School's teaching, and thus the embodiment of the CTLM strategy, is consolidated in a series of teaching team leaders who in turn are directly supervised by the Head. An interesting observation is that the Head refocused his role to be the 'chief leader of teaching' and thus the more traditional School administrative tasks (such as internal organisations, finance, facilities and the like) normally assigned to the Head were delegated to other staff. His reference for such a decision was an extensive meta-analysis that Marzano et. al (2005, pp. 11-27) conducted and which found a .25 correlation between a principal's leadership and student achievement. In simple terms, if focused, the Head's leadership could potentially increase student achievement up to 22% higher than the starting percentile (Marzano et al. 2003, p. 3).

While these aforementioned elements provide an insight into what can be described as the 'visible day to day' elements of the CTLM while in action, it is the elements of 'leadership' and 'school readiness/capacities' which feature prominently, especially in the CTLM's early days, that enable the CTLM to be conceptualised,

---

[9] In the case of this study, data was collected about student performance in literacy using standardised tests in spelling, reading, writing language, conventions and writing capacities.

implemented and refined into the school. We briefly describe and locate each element for reference purposes.

In a previous section we outlined the important role the Head plays in the life of their schools. In the case of the CTLM this is no less so, however the CTLM extends the leadership functions of the school to a designated 'expert teacher' in each teaching team. The 'expert teacher' (the team leader) facilitates the enacting of the CTLM and its associated elements for effect in their teaching team, in what can be described as the 'engine room' of the platform. The term 'expert teacher' is important in the CTLM because this teacher's demonstrated 'expert level teaching capacities' (in other words the performance data for this teacher, on the various metrics used, indicates they have acquired a high capacity to achieve sustained learning outcomes in their students) is pivotal to building the required teaching capacities of the less able teaching team members.

The final element to explain is the 'school's readiness/capacities'. In simple terms this comes to represent a series of considerations and capacities that enable the school, as a whole, to develop, implement, sustain and review the CTLM. These considerations and capacities include things such as an analysis of significant organisational challenges; the required communication mechanisms within the school, a budget, etc, and of course an articulated and agreed School improvement vision. (Fullan and Hargreaves, 2012; Fullan, 2006; Darling-Hammond, 1997) as well as identifying the required first order and second order leadership arrangements (Marzano, et al, 2005).

Having now provided an overview of the CTLM we now review data from the CTLM to provide an insight into the efficacy of such a strategy.

The Study

As we detailed in an earlier section the CTLM focused on the improvement of teaching performance in the curriculum area of English. The school's leadership, through a series of teaching teams, enacted the teaching improvement strategy which is enmeshed in the CTLM, such that teaching performance was measured using student academic achievements in English.

The English curriculum is concerned chiefly with the teaching of spelling, reading, language, writing conventions and genres[10]. To provide a target and a benchmark through which teaching performance could be gauged the Head used Hattie's (2012, 2009, 1999) work, which indicated a teaching effect size of =>0.4 was the desirable teaching effect on student learning. In summary effect-size provides a common expression of the magnitude of study outcomes for all types of outcome variables, such as school achievement. An effect size of $d = 1.0$ indicates an increase of one standard deviation on student achievement. A one standard deviation increase is typically associated with advancing a student's achievement by *two to three years* or *improving the rate of learning by 50%*. When implementing a new program, an effect size of 1.0 would mean that, on average, students receiving that treatment would exceed 84% of those students not receiving that treatment. Hattie (2012, 2009, 1999), having concluded from an extensive meta study of teaching research, proposed that anything with an effect size of over 0.4 is likely to have a visible, positive effect on student achievement. To put it another way, an effect size of 0.2 or less is low, 0.4 is medium and 0.6 or more is high. With these points in mind the Head focused his teachers to achieve >0.4 teaching effect on their students' learning outcomes. The use of standardised tests in English provided an effective means through which to convey such performance to teachers.

---

[10] See http://www.australiancurriculum.edu.au/english/curriculum/f-10?layout=1

To examine the extent to which the CTLM strategy has had an effect on student academic improvements, (Kindergarten through Year 6 or the primary schooling years in Australia) the following research questions are posed:

1. Are there any short-term effects that indicate improved student academic outcomes in English?

2. Using Hattie's d = 0.4 criterion, is there any evidence of better than average student academic outcomes?

3. To what extent can the school project of renewal over five years be related to identified student learning outcomes?

Participants and Context

Consolidating points made earlier about this school we conclude that the selected school is an example of a 'seed' school. These are schools that already have a strong capacity for change, where the staff is cohesive, excited about teaching, led by a visionary leader willing to involve the entire staff in decisions, and broadly aware of research trends and ideas being implemented elsewhere." (Slavin, 1997, p.7). After assuming the position, the Head discerned that the academic performance of students, while above state and sector norms[11], was 'flat-lining'. He resolved to work on creating better academic outcomes (in English as a key curriculum area in the school) by an intensive staff professional development and school structural change project over five years. In what follows, is an account of this approach, which is termed the *Collaborative Teacher Learning Model (CTLM: See also Chapter 2)* and which was implemented over a five-year period. In developing the approach Scheimann's (2014) elements of *Alignment, Capabilities* and *Engagement* have been used to organise and focus key elements

---

[11] Australia's *National Assessment Program for Literacy and Numeracy.*

31

associated with the CTLM. A special emphasis has been placed on (teaching) capabilities.

The school is a large faith-based elementary school located in a regional city in New South Wales, Australia. The school has an average yearly enrolment of 652 elementary students in Years Kindergarten through 6, who are organized into 7 teaching cohorts. The cohorts comprise teams of teachers --- 4 teachers per team and approximately 90 students --- who work collaboratively to deliver the Australian National Curriculum. This teaching arrangement is supported by a 'team leader', a personal teaching performance plan (TPP) for each teacher and a series of formalized coaching, mentoring and feedback sessions managed and facilitated by the team leader. The teaching workforce is relatively stable (staff turnover 12% per year) and contains a mixture of teaching experiences not dissimilar to other schools of its size and location. The student population is representative of the local demographics in that there are no distinguishing features that would make the school's student population different to other schools in its district.

Method

To answer the research questions as posed earlier we analysed literacy standardized test scores. These included the Waddington language tests[12] for which records date back before the renewal process began and the digitization made them available to the research team. We also used scores from the National Assessment Program – Literacy and Numeracy (NAPLAN), the annual assessment for all Australian students in Years 3 and 5. It has been an everyday part of the school calendar since 2008. NAPLAN tests provide point-in-time information about student progress in literacy and numeracy. They are intended to complement the wide range of formal and informal assessments that are already conducted in schools (Board of Studies NSW, 2014). A series of standardised, teacher developed writing tasks (an assessment rubric coupled to a whole of school, leveled and moderated writing task) proved a viable diagnostic tool for teacher planning as well as for gauging increases in each student's overall writing capacities. We also consolidated such findings into effect size gains and report them as overall gains for English writing.

Results

It was possible to examine changes in performance across time for three groups of students: those currently in Year 6 (n=25), Year 5 (n=42) and Year 4 (n=53). Students currently in Year 6 had completed the South Australian (SA) Spelling test on four occasions, in February and November of 2011 and 2012, when they were in Year 3 and in Year 4. Students currently in Year 5 had completed this test on two occasions, when they were in Year 3 in February and November of 2012. Students currently in Year 4, completed this test twice in February and November of 2013.

Figure 2 shows the average performance of these three cohorts of students across these testing occasions adjusted for chronological age (spelling age minus chronological age). It can be seen that students currently in Year 6 had a spelling age slightly above their chronological age at the commencement of Year 3, and that this difference did not change across the academic year (t (24)=0.05, p=. 97). However, when these children were tested again in Year 4 (2012) the difference between their spelling age and chronological age dramatically increased across the academic year (t (24)=3.3, p=. 003).

In that same year, children who are currently in Year 5, and who were at that time in Year 3, also showed evidence of an improvement in their age-adjusted reading performance (t (41)=3.9, p<. 001). Finally, in the following year (2013), children currently in Year 4 had higher adjusted reading ages at the commencement of the year in February, and this differential dramatically increased across the academic year (t (52)=4.3, p<. 001). At the end of 2013, on average, children currently in Year 4 had a reading age approximately 18 months greater than their chronological age.

Figure 2: Average adjusted South Australia spelling age for cohorts of students currently in Year 6, Year 5, or Year 4 for whom data exist for two or more testing occasions[13].

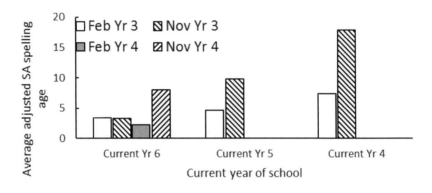

There is also evidence from the Year 3 NAPLAN performance indicating general improvements in literacy levels across the school. Data are available for three cohorts of students completing the Year 3 NAPLAN in 2011, 2012, and 2013. Statistics reported --- following--- are restricted to students in Bands 3 to 6, as inclusion of Bands 1 and 2 results in very small sample sizes in a number of cells, violating the principles of the $\square^2$ test.

Figure 3 shows the percentages of students achieving Band 6 performance in each of the NAPLAN tests (Writing, Language, Reading, and Spelling) for the three-year cohorts. The variations in

---

[13] The adjusted SA spelling age was computed by subtracting the child's chronological age at the time of testing from their spelling age score on that test. Tests were conducted in February, at the commencement of the Australian school year, and in November, at the end of the Australian school year.

proportions of students in each of the four bands of the NAPALN tests evaluated were statistically significant for the Language ($\chi^2_{(6)}$ = 14.57, p = .024) and Writing tests ($\chi^2_{(6)}$ = 12.74, p = .047). They were not significant for Reading ($\chi^2_{(6)}$ = 5.46, p = .486) or for Spelling ($\chi^2_{(6)}$ = 8.258, p = .220).

Changes in performance on the teacher-constructed writing tasks (to test students overall -- cap stone -- writing ability) completed in 2012 and in 2013 were assessed relative to the standard deviation of the initial scores (Term 1 of each year). Figure 4 shows the average performance in the four different tasks on the second occasion of completion relative to the first occasion of completion, expressed as a size of effect (d). It can be seen that in both years the improvement was considerably greater than 0.4.

Figure 3: The percentage of students achieving Band 6 performance in each of the four NAPLAN tests (Writing, Language, Reading and Spelling) completed by Year 3 students in 2011, 2012, and 2013.

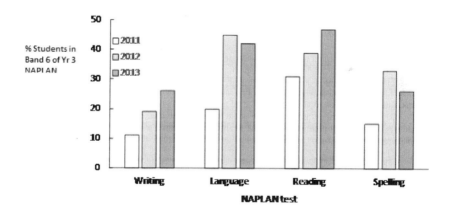

Figure 4: Changes, expressed as size of effect (d), in average performance in the teacher-constructed writing tasks over two administration points in 2012 and 2013.

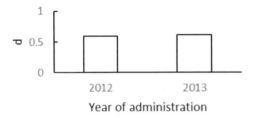

Year of administration

Conclusions

In summary, this study indicates that there are indicative answers to the three research questions posed earlier. First, there is evidence of improved student English outcomes as the Head's strategic intervention progressed. There is clear improvement in English Language and Writing tests according to national criteria in the same period. Second, there is evidence of better than average student academic outcomes indicated by Hattie's *d* criterion in teacher-constructed tests. Three, there is evidence that during the period of intense professional development and concentration on improved student literacy performance outcomes, indicators shifted in a positive direction. It appears that the five-year school renewal has had an effect on student academic performance. This professional development regime reflects the scope of what is outlined in Table 1 (located at chapter's end).

We need to add that the CTLM and the various activities therein, together with the leadership capacities of the Head and his 'team leaders' represent a large body of investigative work, which at the time of writing, still needs to be further investigated. Given this we cannot identify precisely where the effect is located and thus remains part of an ongoing research project. This leads us to further suggest that an extended (and thus scaled-up) version of this seed project into other schools is required (with varying school profiles) to enable a more detailed analysis of the phenomena at play in the CTLM strategy. This work has now commenced.

Having made this statement we do offer the following concluding insights from study anecdotes, which together provide us with a focus for such further investigations.

Schiemann's (2014) ACE model proved an effective means through which the Head was able to communicate his vision for teaching improvement in the school and thus coordinate the various people associated with the CTLM 'on-the-ground' and for us to conceptualise the study. The CTLM and its five inter-related elements (see Table 1 at chapter's end) also proved an effective means through which the Head was able to organise and deliver a comprehensive and aligned professional development program for his teachers and by association to organise the various leadership functions for effect.

Our key point is that while the Head's leadership was a visible and instrumental element within the School and this was reinforced by a closely aligned schema of 'teaching team leaders' --- the engine room if you like of the model --- it appears to us that a clearly outlined framework of how school improvement will take place (AITSL, 2014; Hargreaves and Fullan, 2012; Waters, et al, 2003), together with a coupling of measurable learning outcome data (Young and Kim, 2010; Hattie, 2009; Ansess, et al, 2007) interrogated in a team-based coaching and mentoring arrangement, creates an environment in which overall school improvement can take place (Cordingly and Buckler, 2012; Madden, 2012; Helmer, et al, 2011). In summary the CTLM proves an exemplar of how schools can engage with the 'creating the outstanding school agenda'.

Table 1: Collaborative Teacher Learning Model: Theoretical Elements and Associated References

	Key Theory	Alignment	Capabilities	Engagement
Platform Attributes		*Synchrony of people with the goals, clientele and brand of the organisation, wherever they are located within it.*	*The available knowledge, skill, information and resources available to people sufficient to meet the organisation's goals.*	*Engagement includes people satisfaction, commitment and willingness to take action for the benefit of the organisation in a discretionary way*
School Readiness/ Capacities	Hamel and Zanini (2014), Cochran-Smith, M. & Donnell, K. (2006). Anderson, S. & Kumari, R. (2009). Nuthall, G. (2004). Darling-Hammond, L. (1997). British Educational Research Association. (2014)	Analysis of significant organisational Challenges Problem- solution processes	Inter-personal and intra-organisational communication skills/ mechanisms Strategic Organisational Arrangements	Forthright / Courageous Conversations Forums to discuss strategic issues / feedback progress
Leadership	Marzano,et al (2005) Marzano et al (2003) Leithwood, K., & Jantzi, D. (2000a); (2000b) McWilliam, E. & Haukka, S. (2008 OECD (2013) **Costa, A., & Kallick, B. (1993)** Robinson, V., Hohepa, M., & Lloyd, C. (2009). Purser, S. R., Knight, H. V., & Bedenbaugh, E. H. (1990, April). Leithwood, K. A., Harris, A., & Hopkins, D. (2008). Fullan, M. (2006).	Vision for teaching excellence which is measured by student learning gains. Long Term School Strategic Development Plan	First Order Leadership Second Order Leadership Team-based Leadership	Whole of school community agreements to plans Enrolling Teaching Leaders [Involving teachers at all levels as leaders]

	References			
Coaching, Mentoring and Feedback (Teacher Professional Development mechanism)	Hattie (2009, 2012) Hargreaves and Fullan (2012) Opfer, V & Pedder, D. (2011). Glazer, E. M. & Hannafin, M. J. (2006). Garet, M., Porter, A., Desimone, L., Birman, B., & Yoon, K., (2001) Avalos, B. (2011) Timperley, H., Wilson, R., Barrar, H., & Fung, I. (2009). Borko, H. (2004). AITSL (2014a) AITSL (2014b) Taylor, M, Yates, A. Meyer, L. & Kinsella, P. (2011). Powell, D. R., & Diamond, K. E. (2011). Hipp, K. K., Huffman, J. B., Pankake, A. M. & Olivier, D. F. (2008). Helmer, J., Bartlett, C., Wolgemuth, J. R. & Lea, T. (2011). Zachay, L. J. (2005). Theeboom, Tim., Beersma, Bianca & van Vianen, A. E. M. (2014) Cordingly, P., & Buckler, N. (2012). Blank, S. (2011)	Individual Teacher Performance Audits Teacher Selection Criteria synchronised to the School's Vision especially improving student achievement Team-based Teaching Plans Assigned Teaching Benchmarks and Targets	Defined Teaching Knowledge Base Defined Teaching Competencies	'Round Table' Teaching Planning Meetings' Individual Teacher Professional Development Plans: -Agreed Teaching Targets / strategies / approaches and associated teacher Professional development elements -Scaled Teaching Performance Measures -Benchmarked Teaching Performance Assigned Coach and Mentor Strategic Professional Develop for each teacher
Performance Data (Standardised Testing Regime Data Management System)	Hattie (2009, 2012) Nisbett (2005) Ancess et al (2007) Rodwell and Sale (2007) Stronge, J. H., Ward, T. J., & Grant, L. W. (2011). Young and Kim (2010) Schildkamp, K. and Kuiper, W., (2010) Tolley, H. and Shulruf, B., (2009) Blau, I. and Presser, O. (2013	Focus on one core curriculum area to start the cycle of improvement Making explicit instructional strategy requirements Data collection regime / reporting regime Diagnostics focused regime of testing	Data / trend analysis of student academic achievement Diagnostics	Whole of School Student Learning Performance Reports Readily accessible data reports in diagnostic formats

3. Preparing Your School for Data Driven Change

Jake Madden

External accountability measures by governments and educational authorities alike have placed school leaders under pressure to improve teaching and learning. This chapter outlines how school leaders can use a data driven approach to improve teacher performance. Furthermore, the chapter outlines the essential elements for its development in schools and how to begin the process.

This chapter outlines a series of essential elements for fostering a data driven culture within a school. While the elements are presented in a linear fashion for discussion purposes they are in fact elements that require each other for effect. These elements include; establishing a vision for change, securing staff commitment, building required processes, facilities and arrangements, designing and enacting sustainable professional learning activities and enacting approaches to school-wide leadership that directs, nourishes and sustains a 'data focused teaching and learning agenda'.

However, I hasten to add and thus highlight that the 'foundation stone' of any change agenda in a school is the school leader. They in effect need to be the 'champion' of such a data driven agenda, but also competent with the associated processes and cognoscente of what findings mean for teaching effect and how same informs remedial and developmental strategies.

Introduction

In Chapter 1 the premise of a Knowledge Economy was outlined. The term proves a convenient way of explaining the changed world in which teachers now teach and students thus learn. With the advent of technological innovation and the globalisation of economies, schools are increasingly having to think about how best to prepare students for the opportunities and challenges that a Knowledge Economy represents.

On a related plane, each teacher's teaching performance, through various national testing regimes, is being scrutinized. 'Data' is awash in schools and the challenge for Schools is working out what it all means and finding the time to process it for learning outcomes effect.

A study into the use of data by teachers in two American districts (Ikemoto & Marsh, 2007) indicated that it was not being fully utilized or exploited by teachers for teaching improvement. Where it was utilsed it appeared to only result in or be used to inform peripheral decision making in the school (i.e. timetable changes, identifying topics for the next professional development round, or providing information for annual reports). Further, data was not interrogated to any depth. Research appears to also suggest that teachers and principals think connecting student achievement to decision-making is tenuous and complicates an already busy school/ classroom operation (Ikemoto & Marsh, 2007; Hargreaves, 2007; William, 2007/2008). So, although educational policy makers purport that student achievement will be systematically increased as a result of micro and macro decisions driven by data, the reality is yet to be realised.

On a related plane, An Institute of Education Sciences Expert Panel report (Hamilton et al., 2009) examined nearly 500 studies where instructional strategies were implemented based on teachers and leaders examination of school related data. Only 64 of these studies used "experimental, quasi-experimental, and single subject designs to examine whether data use leads to increases in student achievement" and only 6 studies highlighted grounds for data driven decisions improving student achievement (Hamilton et al., 2009, p1). Such research leads to the conclusion that teachers using data driven instruction to raise student achievement is yet to be fully realized in schools.

While schools have always used data sources to report to authorities and stakeholders, using it to guide teacher practice is in its infancy. Shifting the common teacher 'view' that such external measures are just an aspect of external bureaucracy is perhaps the inherent challenge.

From my own experiences using a data driven decision-making process in a school 'requires' organizational capacity and a teacher skilling program for such an agenda to become instrumental in classroom and school-wide decision making.

So what is a data driven decision making approach and how is it enabled?

Data Driven Focus

Data-driven decision-making is the systematic process of collecting, analyzing, and synthesizing 'data', from a variety of sources and then making corresponding teaching decisions. There is a direct interface in the data process with the development of the classroom curriculum in that such 'decisions' come to frame and inform what the teacher does next. In Chapter 5 the premise of this data driven environment is further explained through an outlining of the Collaborative Teacher Learning Model. This model exemplifies what I outline in this chapter as a 'whole of school teaching improvement model'. There are five elements that inform the premise of the data driven schools: They are

1.   Driven Leaders
The leadership of the school shapes the culture of the school. Data driven decision-making needs to be incorporated and supported not

only by the school leaders, but also the 'middle managers' and teacher leaders. The organizational practices of the school must support and engage actions that are formulated from using data analysis. Leaders who seek data and demonstrate to staff how the data influences and forms future programs and practices help staff understand the connection of using data to inform decision making.

2. Multiple Data Sources:

A prerequisite for informing instructional practice for teachers is to have an understanding of the need to use reliable and valid sources of data. Reliance on a single (ie a national standardized test), narrow or 'one-off' set to inform one's teaching practice is limiting.

3. Teacher Centred Data Collection Tools:

To improve instructional practice teachers need to have 'at their fingertips' data collected from their classrooms. They need to be able to analyse daily the results of their instruction and thus need the appropriate tools to capture data. Too often schools are focused on collecting data and delivering it to teachers rather than enabling and skilling teachers to generate/ manage their own data on students and their teaching performance.

4. Train Your Teachers:

As we move into this new era of teaching and learning, it is necessary to train teachers to not only analyse and understand student data but also be able to respond appropriately to it. Preparing teachers to use data is a key step to building their capacity as effective educators. The job embedded professional development approach, the use of an instructional coach and the learning community approach will help teachers focus on creating the links between curricula, teaching strategies and assessment.

5. Daily Data Driven Instruction:

School leaders need to make explicit that data driven instruction is a daily part of the teaching and learning process. It should be viewed as 'regular professional practice': not the latest fad. All professions engage with data and teachers are perhaps just late bloomers. Making the connection between analyzing data, integrating it into planning and then implementing the targeted teaching strategies need to be seamless and automatic. Simply put, teachers need to be able to articulate why they are using a particular strategy for the specific group of students.

In summary, a data driven mindset builds a teachers' capacity to meet the learning needs of each individual student. Inherent in building a model for using data in a school is thus the need to include guidelines for collecting, processing and analyzing data and enacting feedback and planning decisions to close the loop on what the data comes to mean.

Data Driven Decision Making In Acton

Given this need to link structures and building upon the five essential elements outlined earlier, and in reference to my own experience in such work (Madden, 2012) a model for enacting same can be outlined as:

1. Developing Desire
2. Creating Space for Conversation
3. Building a Data Driven Decision Making Cycle
4. Engaging in Distributed Leadership
5. Formative Feedback Practices
6. Job Embedded Professional Development

A brief explanation of these building blocks follow:

1. Developing A Desire for Change…..
Establishing a vision for a 'preferred future' is the initial task for the school leader in any change process: but getting traction to implement the vision is the next challenge. However, leaders need staff 'buy in': to not only engage in the change process but also ensure the agenda's sustainability. In explaining to staff what is changing and why, the school leader needs to show staff where the school is positioned today and where the vision intends to position them tomorrow. The key to building a desire for change is to make

sure staff understand why this matters to the school and to them and how such changes will positively impact their roles, career plans and (most importantly) how the school will measure its success. My point is that data (i.e. staff satisfaction surveys, departmental action plans and evidence gained from classroom assessments and the like) builds the platform for shaping a staff's focus on the need for change.

2.   *Creating Space for Conversation….*

The school leader is responsible for creating not only time to engage teachers in the process of working with student achievement data but also the physical spaces in which to work with it. In simple terms the premise of working with data means the work environment and the associated facilities for teachers will also need a rethink. This is a comment about how different work practices often require 'different' work environments.

At my current school, as principal, I have instituted a 'staff hub' as a dedicated space where data and support facilities are 'housed'. I am also exploring the use of 'hand held data devices' to enable ready data usage. In short, creating a space where innovation, creativity and brainstorming around the key elements is an enabler for teachers. The 'staff hub' also provides a space for:

- Instructional leadership to flourish and allow open dialogue between teachers and school leaders.
- Teachers to plan their instruction after analysing data. Coupled with reorganizing school timetables to arrange grade teachers' blocks of planning time, having such discussion leads to the agreement of targeted intervention strategies. Teachers are able to collaborate with peers to hone their instructional strategies.
- Conversations on data, which tends to focus the "school day" and inculcate teachers to anaylsing and talking about what they do.

3.   *Building A Data Driven Decision Making Cycle….*

Understanding the process of data decision making is a central skill teachers must develop in order to make effective decisions about instructional directions in their classroom. The school leader needs to inculcate within each teacher the capacity to not only collect and analyse data, but interpret the data in such a fashion that it leads to effective decision making on the instructional interventions needed to address students' learning needs. Consequently, successful decision-making is not simply applying a prescribed formula to learning but more strategically personalized to the nuances of the individual learner/ teacher.

Using what is termed an 'action research cycle' (see Timperley, 2005), the key steps established during my tenures as a school leader, in making effective instructional decisions using data, include:

a.   Be clear on information needed
b.   Administer assessments and collect relevant data
c.   Critique and analyse data sets
d.   Establish learning priorities and set key attainment goals
e.   Identify and implement appropriate teaching strategies
f.   Reflect on success

This scaffolding and provision of guidelines for professional teacher discussions on data collection, analysis and intervention also assists in improving teacher practice. It offers a neat structure for feedback sessions between classroom teacher and mentor.

4.   *Engaging in Distributed Leadership….*

Schools are social institutions. Engaging in leadership practices that are focused upon teams of teachers rather than individual teachers operating 'in their own closed teaching world' supports both staff and students. On a pragmatic level, one leader, especially in a large diverse school, cannot do all the work that school improvement requires. Consequently, the need to foster leadership that is distributed through teaming is a key organizational and sustainability strategy (Crowther and Ferguson, 2009; Gronn, 2000; Katzenmeyer & Moller, 2001).

Building and sustaining a culture of what I call 'teacher leadership' requires shared understandings and of course further skilling. Furthermore, building leadership capacity within the school's staff is another process in building overall school capacity (Ebmeier & Nicklaus, 1999) which in turns impacts positively on school improvement.

5.   *Formative Feedback Practices….*
Pivotal to sustaining the data driven culture is the use of formative feedback structures that allow leaders and teachers to interact and thus communicate/ support movements towards this student achievement regime. The key to these feedback sessions is the use of 'processed data' ---graphs are good examples---which makes simple yet effective comparisons or provides key insights into what is happening as a result of a teachers teaching. In my case as a school leader three important principles guide the feedback to teachers in both formal and informal settings. Teachers need:

a.   Knowledge of what 'outstanding teaching performance' is. Continually referring to what constitutes an outstanding lesson or effective preparation, planning and programming keeps the focus on high expectations and continual improvement.

b.   The capability to compare how their current teaching performance relates to outstanding teaching performance. With regular meetings between Heads of Departments/Year Level Leaders and the classroom teacher, making distinctions between the results of recent lesson observations and the ideal outstanding lesson helps identify areas of improvement.

c.   Knowledge of how to reduce the gap between their current classroom performance and the goal of an outstanding teaching performance. This is the 'Holy Grail' for the classroom teacher. Using the feedback on teaching practice, classroom teachers use the appropriate teaching strategies needed to improve their own teaching. Aligning the strategies to target student achievement needs also highlights teacher needs for improvement.

6.   *Job Embedded Professional Development….*

Coupled with the formative feedback mechanisms developed for improving teacher practice and the examining of student achievement results, teachers and leaders alike need targeted professional development. While attending workshops away from the classroom are good in early stages, an embedded approach through coaching, mentoring and feedback by the competent and experienced 'data user' is an important strategy. In my own experience I have found teaming up with a University's education faculty has enabled this type of capacity to be seeded into the school.

Conclusion

The role of leaders in creating a data driven culture is a key step in turning data into knowledge practical enough for teachers to use to improve student learning.

Beginning with developing the desire for change, the school leader establishes the vision and then sets about connecting that vision to the programs, processes and expectations of the school. The importance of staff ownership of the change process and the setting up of a data driven decision-making cycle/ mechanism/ facility helps to build leadership capacity in all teachers and sets the culture of data driven decision making into action. The effective leader nurtures the data driven culture by building the necessary infrastructures throughout the school to facilitate the implementation of data driven decision-making.

The underlying challenge in focusing on building a data driven school is to adhere to the research on school improvement. Simply put, the greatest influence on student outcomes is the classroom teacher (Hargreaves & Fullan, 2012; Darling-Hammond & Rothman, 2011; Hattie, 2008). Consequently increasing student attainment needs school leaders to be aggressively engaged in fostering and directing teacher improvement. In simple terms becoming data experts doesn't automatically mean teachers become expert teachers. Data decision making is but a key means to an end.

4. Coaching, Mentoring and Feedback: What do they mean for Education?

Richard Smith and David Lynch

The teaching profession has a common aspiration to improve the quality of student learning outcomes through teaching. Being able to do this is an important part of a teacher's professional identity and at the heart of such an aspiration is for all stduents to make the required learning gains. The challenge is knowing how to sustainably build teaching capacity in a school. This chapters examines the concepts of coaching, mentoring and feedback as one such strategy.

As earlier chapters have indicated, the teaching profession has a common aspiration to improve the quality of student learning outcomes through teaching. Being able to do this is an important part of a teacher's professional identity. These pressures weigh heavily not just on teachers, but on school heads and middle management as well who have the added responsibility to lead a systematic approach to the requirements in ways that improve effective teaching (Smith and Lynch, 2010).

Continuing the theme of models to enact the outstanding school, in this chapter we explore the concepts of coaching , mentoring and feedback as they relate to education. You will recall in Chapter 1 how these three inter-rlated elements featured prominently in the Collaborative Teacher Learning Model. In this chapter we review the literature to better understand each. First we turn to teacher education for points of reference.

First to Teacher Education

The history of teacher education has a lot to do with the present search for ways to build effective schools and to improve the performance of teaching (Lynch, 2012). Following much of the American agenda of 'objective' methods created by people such as Thorndike, the psychological approach became the accepted standard for educational research in Australia by the 1960s (Lagemann, 1996). It was supplemented by the efficiency movement in educational management and by a division of labour that separated teachers from university researchers (Darling-Hammond, 1997).

Two effects followed. First, the objective methods precisely produced knowledge that is abstract, without context and focused on practice and that cannot be integrated into classrooms. Teachers, then, tend to ignore 'research' because it is difficult to apply to their daily work. Second, two professional communities --- or 'tribes' --- were produced, namely university researchers and school practitioners (Menter, 2011; Smith, 2000) which distinguish 'headwork' from 'manual labour'. Even today, the legacy of university researchers inventing knowledge for teachers to apply has currency and continues to affect the ways in which teaching in teacher education degrees is done and accreditation processes are conceived and administered (Smith and Lynch, 2010). The socio-cultural demands on schooling exacerbate the impact of the legacy and complicate the need for change.

Such dilemmas and solutions are hardly restricted to Education (Smith and Lynch, 2010). For instance, Paquette (2012) proposes that museum operations are very different from what they were only a decade or so ago. They are now considered as agents of social inclusion and social change, suggesting a change in organizational culture in which museums must change their focus to the social agenda of museums and to social engagement in the museums. The parallel with teaching, nursing and many other professions is apparent. All of them face pressures to 'change', generated by a common background of social, cultural, economic and political movement, generically described as 'globalisation'.

What emerges from these over-arching pressures are serious organisational questions that are often unrecognised in their entirety by observers and commentators. Whether it is schools, universities, businesses or museums, these institutions have socialized and created leaders and other staff in different educational experiences and values, and for decades used leadership selection criteria that have an uneasy fit with current conditions. With new broad social and political demands, the search is on for ways to influence and change organizational culture where leaders normally champion and use orthodox, received cultural mores. There is a strengthening trend to think of the workforce more as an important source of competitive advantage requiring new leadership skills rather than dealing with other traditional leadership roles, such as financial resources, technology, or economies of scale (Pfeffer, 1994 in Kroth and Keeler, 2009). In addition and more importantly, if these new policy goals and mandates are to be established as the new orthodoxy, a new workforce and leadership is required. In the Education sector, the challenge for schools, heads and teachers then is how to do it (Sachs and Parsell, 2014; Lynch, 2012).

In recent years, mentoring has become a feature of the business world, where it is used in the induction of new staff into the culture of the organization, to improve communication between different levels of management, and to encourage access for traditionally excluded groups from senior management positions. The interest in other professions such as Medicine, Nursing, and Education has followed.

Mentoring and Coaching

In this section, we canvas arguments across the literature that capture the core issues and challenges in which the terms 'mentoring' and 'coaching' are embedded. Mentoring has ancient origins, but modern day mentoring has roots in the European apprenticeship system, when the apprentice learnt skills from the master craftsman (Clutterbuck, 1985). This legacy led to many images of 'mentoring' that reflect the difficulty of exact definition (see Carter, 2013; DfES, 2005). While coaching in an organizational sense has traditionally been viewed as a way to correct poor performance and to link individual effectiveness with organizational performance (Ellinger et al., 2003), the distinction between coaching and mentoring has not been clear.

The categorisation difficulty in this field is captured by Hamlin, Ellinger, and Beattie (2008) who conducted a comprehensive literature review and identified 37 coaching definitions. They created four broad variants labelled "coaching," "executive coaching," "business coaching," and "life coaching." The key issue is that the coaching process of providing help to individuals, groups, and organizations through some form of 'facilitation activity or intervention' was found to be common to all four variants (Beattie et al., 2014, 186). Thus, all variants were based on:

> … the explicit and implicit intention of helping individuals to improve their performance in various domains, and to enhance their personal effectiveness, personal development, and personal growth (Hamlin et al., 2008, p. 291).

Organizations and the literature use the terms mentoring and coaching interchangeably. More specifically, coaching and formal mentoring are similar in nature but different in name (Joo, Sushko and McLean, 2012 p. 30). We follow this advice except where either mentoring or coaching is the core of the discussion.

In addition, the construct teacher 'professional development' (PD) can be rendered as Continuing Professional Development (CPD), teacher learning, school improvement and so on. In each of them, mentoring and coaching play a key role in their implementation. We thus refer to both PD and CPD as generic terms in what follows.

At the outset, it is important to note that there are only a few studies on managerial coaching (Gilley et al. 2010; Park 2007) and fewer empirical studies about the outcomes of managerial coaching and mentoring that have definitive results (Beattie et al. 2014, p. 188). In particular, there is a dearth of studies about the direct and indirect associations between managerial coaching and mentoring where employee responses have been studied. In addition, Paustian-Underdahl et al. (2013) indicate, "little is known about the factors that may play a role in supervisors' supportiveness" (p. 290) and the characteristics of highly supportive supervisors.

Nevertheless, the literature does corroborate common themes for effective coaching and mentoring behaviours in schools including creating a learning environment, caring and supporting staff, providing feedback, communicating, and providing resources including other people. These are reflected in the DfES (2005) statement that provides the following definitions for an education context.

- Mentoring is a structured, sustained process for supporting professional learners through significant career transitions;

- Specialist Coaching is a structured, sustained process for enabling the development of a specific aspect of a professional learner's practice;

- Collaborative (Co-) Coaching is a structured, sustained process between two or more professional learners to enable them to embed new knowledge and skills from specialist sources in day-to-day practice.

Hamlin et al. (2006, p. 326) conclude that "truly effective managers and managerial leaders are those who embed effective coaching into the heart of their management practice". Cordingly and Buckler (2012) make the point that for those studies showing a "positive impact on both teacher and learner outcomes" of mentoring and coaching, the most important messages are the processes involved:

collaboration, sustained, embedded in real-life learning contexts, and supported by specialists.

Normally, 'mentoring' refers to a one-to-one relationship in an organization where a senior experienced person or specialist offers guidance, help, support and advice to facilitate the learning or development of a junior or less experienced other. Curiously, based on management research in nursing, education, and management, Kroth and Keeler (2009) argue that contemporary managerial strategies and models do not adequately address the importance of 'caring' between managers and employees.

Paquette (2012) identifies three literatures in the mentoring field. In the *sociological literature*, mentoring is an act of social reproduction as a mentor, based on knowledge, experience, or symbolic capital, transmits information, strategies, social capital, and prestige that are necessary for institutional change and career progression. Those mentored in such an arrangement become the legitimate heirs to the mentor, a view that fits an interpretation of mentoring as a conservative practice reminiscent of medieval apprenticeship, reproducing and communicating the 'tricks of the trade'.

There is a 100-year old literature about schooling as the social reproduction of the class structure and the baleful effects of professional cultures that stifle innovation. In Paquette's (2012, p. 209) view, "most of the literature—even the most supportive of mentoring—conveys the idea that mentoring is equivalent to normalization and social reproduction or learning as an uncritical engagement with a body of professional or organizational knowledge". The mentoring concept must overcome this legacy in practice if it is to have any impact on the constraints and restraints that it purports to transform.

The *managerial literature*, emphasizes formal mentoring and the mutual benefits of relationships for both organisations and the mentored. The idea that employees and their manager work for the organisation and therefore coaching and mentoring are tools to assist this process, is hardly questioned. The third approach then is that of an emergent practice in which a new professional seeks or receives *"advice and guidance"* for his or her career from a senior colleague through a 'durable relationship' (Paquette, 2012).

Summarising Paquette's survey, the literature conveys the idea that mentoring is an experience that involves a single mentor, but that this characteristic is an artefact of the kinds of research that have been done rather then a conceptual or theoretical position. The second issue is that the literature emphasizes the processes of normalization. "This characteristic is quite salient in the sociological works; it is the desired outcome of the managerial stream of the literature and is a core component of the vocational one—especially from the psycho-social point of view" (Paquette, 2012, p. 209). Paquette concludes that the potential of mentoring for creativity and potential innovation is underestimated so that the idea is rarely associated with organizational and institutional change. This is an important cue for those in education where school reform and more effective teaching to produce improved student academic outcomes are the main game.

The term 'mentor' usually invokes the idea of a formal relationship between an experienced worker and a less experienced one, but the literature shows that in today's work climate involving the need for changed work patterns and cohorts of people, traditional hierarchal mentoring relationships are ineffective. Different forms of mentoring have evolved to fit the circumstances: including peer mentoring, co-mentoring, developmental alliances, situational or spot mentoring that is short term and goal specific, 'mentoring up' in which senior employees are mentored by junior employees, team and group mentoring, and e-mentoring" (Mavrinac, 2005).

However well intentioned, attempts to restrict the scope and range of mentoring and coaching are, it seems, doomed. Kram (1985) and Roche (1979) describe both informal and formal modes of mentoring. Caruso's (1989) study in a business setting showed that professional and emotional support came from a number of sources rather than one formal mentor. In this way, mentoring can be a relationship between colleagues, where their respective status is equal and communication is two-way. Reflecting this reality, Kram and Isabella (1985) identify a continuum of peer relationships: Information Peer, Collegial Peer, and Special Peer. Kram (1985) identifies two main areas of support provided by the mentoring relationship. Career development includes sponsorship, visibility, exposure, coaching, protection, and challenging assignments while the psychosocial includes role-modelling, friendship, counselling, acceptance and confirmation. While categories such as 'coaching' are identified as discrete entities, the term 'mentoring' fuses them into a single superordinate concept.

These two areas of support, mentoring and coaching, are fundamental in school settings where professional development is inextricably linked with the personal history of the individual teachers involved. Each teacher has a personal angle on 'teaching' and teaching style, determined by accumulated knowledge and ideas, perceptions of the profession, and era in which they undertook teacher education (Lynch and Smith, 2012). Bringing this enormous array of differences and similarities to the table for disciplined dialogue is a priority for school leaders where the psychosocial functions present special challenges. As an illustration, St-Jean and Audet (2013) report that an intervention style that combines a *maieutic approach* [aspect of the Socratic method that induces a respondent to formulate latent concepts through a dialectic or logical sequence of questions] with mentor involvement enabled the mentor to play a more decisive role with the mentee, indicating that mentors need to be able to vary their approach. Mentoring and coaching are a very diverse church indeed.

Nevertheless, the mentoring role is fraught not just for school leaders. Spaten and Flensborg's (2013) study of 15 middle managers trained to coach 75 employees found that the manager as coach has to be sensitive and empathetic in building the coaching relationship and should draw clear boundaries between their role as leader with a power relationship and supportive coach. Seibert (2013) in a study of 11 companies and 5,000 employees reports that where employees believed that their managers provided ongoing coaching and feedback to help them succeed, 93% reported a willingness to put in additional effort when needed, compared to only 33% of those who reported poor coaching and feedback. If this study is representative, it suggests that mentoring and coaching skills are a core capability for leaders and that even then, the processes can go wrong.

There is a clear trend in the literature away from 'management' emphases towards what might be called a 'Human Relations' approach. It has emerged as an important area for leadership where immediate managers or coaches are in a pivotal position to optimize people 'investments' (Schiemann, 2011). In this approach, human capital is central to achieving the mission and goals of the organization, another way of saying that employees matter and that the organisation and management have a responsibility to optimise both training and work conditions. In turn, dealing with 'alignment', 'capabilities', and 'engagement' of people, are central to the optimization of human capital investments and maximising overall organisational performance (Schiemann, 2011). While education staff may baulk at the lexicon of such work, there are many instructive concepts in this literature for both the application of mentoring and coaching processes and for asking pertinent research questions about PD.

Pausing for a moment, nowhere does the gravity of PD weigh more heavily on leadership, management and staff than in education institutions. As the pressures to improve teaching and student outcomes increase, school heads are daily faced with issues such as how teachers and middle managers can be most effective at work, how their commitment to common goals determined both beyond the school and within can be encouraged and sustained. To participate in disciplined dialogue (Swaffield & Dempster, 2009), mentoring becomes an essential technique as it offers an approach to both the work place individual and the personal side of human development in so far as individuals can be helped to explore their potential. Hence, mentoring is about the whole of an individual's relationship to work and the ability to thrive within it rather than the transmission of a limited set of skills, important as these may be in some circumstances. The Human Relations approach, perhaps stripped of some its imposing terminology that may well threaten the sensibilities of educators, offers a resource to perceptive education leaders.

To illustrate the point, here are some examples. In a business environment, coaching recipients report satisfaction with the experience for developing intrapersonal and interpersonal areas, especially self-efficacy (Theeboom, Beersma, Bianca, van Vianen, and Annelies (2014). Susing and Cavanagh (2013) point out that career developmental stages as well as personality traits have clear but distinct empirical links to work-based performance. What is more, the mentoring concept and process appears to be transferable to other contexts.

In their study of workplace stress, Yang, Liu-Qin, Xu, Xian, Allen, Tammy, Shi, Kan, Zhang, Xichao and Lou, Zhongyan (2011) found that Chinese business employees understood mentoring relationships in a way similar to Western employees, indicating that the concept is valid in a Confucian culture. Similarly, in his review of eight Education studies from 1997 to 2007 selected from the ERIC and Education Complete databases, Hsiu-Lien Lu (2010) found that peer coaching appears to possess unique advantages and have much value for preservice teacher education, while Smith & Ingersoll, (2004), Portner (2008), Stanulis & Floden, (2009) conclude that mentoring constitutes a vital tool in providing support for new teachers during induction to the profession.

On their part, Cordingly and Buckler (2012, p. 221) state that CPD is most effective when it is "collaborative, sustained, embedded in real-life learning contexts, and supported by specialists" and that mentoring and coaching provide "tailor-made in-school strategies". The mentoring concept appears robust and, for all intents and purposes, is universal in PD settings.

From management to staff capacity

Traditionally, as Leithwood, Harris and Hopkins (2008) point out, school leaders have been reasonably successful at influencing working conditions and fostering motivation and commitment amongst school staff, but under the pressures of the demands noted earlier, they have had a relatively weak influence on building staff capacity: arguably the 'old' agenda in today's circumstances. Following Swaffield & MacBeath's (2009) notion that leadership is an activity rather than a position, the school head's role in professional development of all staff implies a strong organisational component, a strong influence over priorities within a school's professional learning program for teachers and middle managers and the ability to make things happen (Timperley, 2009). As indicated earlier, the 'how' part of the job has become a major determinant of the head's success or failure and now encompasses managerial, Human Relations and 'business' insights into how to lead a contemporary education organisation in both the public and non-government sectors. School heads in particular also need to monitor progress and adjust processes in order to maintain continuing forward momentum, implying a systematic use of data collection and interpretation as part of the core work schedule. In short, a school leader has a pivotal responsibility for providing the optimal conditions so that time is created for critical professional friendships to develop, and for the mentorship and coaching of staff to occur.

Swaffield & Dempster's (2009) concept of 'disciplined dialogue' is helpful for understanding the school leader's relationships with middle managers and in turn their relationship with teachers. Fowler (2012) emphasises the point that disciplined dialogue is based on real data that are critical to understanding teaching, students and their learning rather than hearsay, anecdote or rumour. An important process to achieve these outcomes is referred to as 'mentoring'.

A necessary capability for school leaders in the future is the capacity to improve the effectiveness of instructional practice (Fowler, 2012), an issue to which this review will return later. Once this is accepted then it follows that school leaders need, as a central tenet of their professional repertoire, the knowledge and skill base to make decisions about the impact of teaching on student learning outcomes. Moreover, in order to do this, school leaders need to focus much of their effort on the core business of teaching and learning (Robinson, Hohepa and Lloyd 2010) so that middle managers and teachers also have a heightened awareness of the importance of inquiring into the impact of their teaching on student academic outcomes. When teachers develop their own inquiry skills and can apply them, it is more likely that there will be sustained improvement in teaching effectivness (BERA, 2013; Timperley, Wilson, Barrar and Fung 2009). Thus, as MacBeath and Dempster (2009) point out, the teaching role is delineated as delivering a curriculum, but with systematic inquiry into curriculum and the art and science of teaching. For contemporary teachers, these concepts constitute professional knowledge, and leadership that leads to a successful amalgam of these at the teacher level is all about capacity building (Smith and Lynch, 2010).

Kram (1985), in a study of ten teachers, found that the role of the head teacher, the role of colleagues and the ethos of the school were significant in providing teaching support. Drawing on Kram's work, the ethos of the school depends on the vision of the head teacher and the commitment of colleagues. The head teacher is presented by Kram's data as a figurehead and, at the same time, the founder or the vision behind the culture of the school. This is important as Carter's (2013) research showed. Elements of peer mentoring could be identified in a culture where staff were committed to the vision and had a fundamental belief in what they were doing. The individuals were able to identify strongly with the group and with the collective beliefs and along with colleagues, reflect upon their experiences. The review will deal with the 'reflection' construct later.

Several characteristics appear vital for a successful school head mentor. They include taking a personal interest in the professional well-being of staff, modelling and fostering high standards and expectations, behaviours in their head teachers which are regarded as inspiring such as ability to motivate, knowledge of educational theory and practice, personality and leadership qualities, judgment and trust. In short, "[A] mentor relationship is a two-way street. To make it work, you have to bring something to the party" (Blank, 2011). To reinforce Blank's categories, Ellinger et al. (2003) created coaching behaviour measures that identified eight themes: (1) personalizing learning situations, (2) broadening employees' perspectives-- getting them to see things differently (3) question framing to encourage employees to think through issues (4) stepping into other's shoes to shift perspectives (5) providing feedback to employees, (6) soliciting feedback from employees (7) setting and communicating expectations and (8) being a resource.

Several aspects of what is required in principle appear regularly in the literature. They include the influence of colleagues as peers who provide a range of specific supportive techniques. Crucially, their commitment to the culture of the school is a core ingredient for a successful mentoring program over time, and all mentoring programs are long, rather than short-term projects. Appropriate culture initiates the continuing self-motivation and support that enables the mentored to grow in confidence and take control of their own development.

Confirming other studies cited here, confidence, self-esteem, self-efficacy are all factors that emerge in the mentoring process and contribute to personal and professional development. Gong, Chen and Yang (2014) showed that mentoring mechanisms like these have a sustained influence on personal learning and career outcomes. Their study of 246 business context employees indicated that mentoring mediates the effect between personal learning and career outcomes. Nevertheless, in another business environment study, Kim, Egan, Kim, and Kim (2013, p 325) report a study of direct and indirect effects of managerial coaching behaviour on employee role clarity, work attitudes, and performance. They claim that it is one of the first studies to provide evidence for the influence of managerial coaching behaviour on employee role cognition, work attitudes, and performance. They also point out that there is no commonly acknowledged theory or conceptual model for managerial coaching outcomes and, to date, they were unable to identify any study of managerial coaching in Asian cultural contexts.

By way of summary, it is worth quoting in full from the study by Ingvarson et al. (2005). This snippet contains elements of all of the features of PD mentioned so far and puts the emphasis on what the teachers want and do with the resources they receive.

> … the most effective programs, in terms of reported impact, had profiles consistent with research on effective professional development … They were rated highly by teachers across all five opportunity to learn measures in the conceptual model … They provided opportunities for teachers to focus on what students were to learn and how to deal with the problems students may have in learning that subject matter. They focused on research-based knowledge about student learning of content. They included opportunities for teachers to examine student work collaboratively and in relation to standards for what the students in question should know and be able to do. They led teachers to actively reflect on their practice and compare it with high standards for professional practice. They engaged them in identifying what they needed to learn, and

in planning the learning experiences that would help them meet those needs. They provided time for teachers to test new teaching methods and to receive follow-up support and coaching in their classrooms as they faced problems of implementing changes. (Ingvarson et al., 2005, p.15)

The Issues for Education

In this section, we present a number of matters and issues that affect the conceptualisation, understanding, use and research about mentoring and coaching in Education. There is no particular order in the presentation although the first matter, 'teacher professional learning' is clearly of prime importance. It encapsulates all of the other issues mentioned and discussed in this review and provides a rough, indicative framework for gaining a 'bird's-eye' view of schools undertaking fundamental --- dare we say radical ---- changes.

Issue #1: Changing Teacher Behaviour

There are three systems involved in teacher professional learning: the individual teacher, the school, and the activities (Opfer and Pedder, 2011). The individual teacher system encompasses their prior experiences, their orientation to, and beliefs about, learning, their prior knowledge, and how these are enacted in their classroom practice. School-level systems involve the contexts of the school that support teaching and learning, the collective orientations and beliefs about learning, the collective practices or norms of practice that exist in the school, and the collective capacity to realize shared learning goals (Lynch and Smith, 2011). Finally, because the focus is teacher professional learning, the systems of learning activities, tasks, and practices in which teachers take part are included.

Opfer and Pedder's (2011) work has important implications. They restate the findings of previous research that indicate: how and what a teacher learns is strongly influenced by orientation to learning, that the perceptions and beliefs of teachers are the most significant predictors of change, and that these are not easily altered. They emphasise that of the studies specifically aimed at changing teacher orientations to learning with course work and learning activities, few have been successful. Moreover, teachers are more likely to embrace evidence supporting their existing orientations than evidence that contradicts them (Tillema, 2000; Chinn & Brewer, 1993).

This is a highly relevant issue for mentoring and coaching because teacher education strategies have typically encouraged the development of an individualized personal teaching approach by student teachers as the legitimate role of teacher education programs, and such an orientation is expected in practising teachers. High value is placed on teachers explicitly discussing, elaborating and constructing their own beliefs (Tillema, 2000). Several difficulties follow.

First, it is difficult, if not impossible to link pre-existent lay theories and student teachers beliefs to contemporary knowledge on teaching without creating such great diversity, incoherence, and sometimes even conflict, between the knowledge bases that presenting an accepted knowledge base to student teachers is fraught (Tillema, 2000). Second, even personal belief systems about teaching are severely challenged and overruled by the preconditions set by practice. One might also expect that as 'experience' in such conditions increases, belief systems are reinforced and sustained.

Tillema's (2000) third point is that in the face of practice, student teachers often feel unable to reconcile their own beliefs with what is experienced, and that experience 'puts them in a position in which they feel inadequately prepared and ill-equipped to do what is expected of them'. In short, there are serious difficulties that block a teacher's capacity *to construct their own reflective belief system* at the beginning of a career and in the on-going work situation.

Amongst his conclusions, Tillema (2000) reports:

The meaningfulness of reflection depends upon the prevalent performance repertoire, not just upon the beliefs, which previously existed. This underscores the primacy of *practice* over beliefs, and reflection *as adding to the experiences already acquired in practice*, thus establishing a conceptual congruence between behaviour and thinking.

Tillema's study particularly challenges the notion of encouraging pre- and post-initial teacher education participants to 'reflect' before practice, one of the dominant strategies in teacher education, because it is prone to the creation of incongruity between beliefs and performance.

Issue #2: Creation and Sharing of Knowledge

A major issue in the teacher professional development literature is what is understood by the 'creation and sharing of knowledge' and how it can be achieved and researched. In addition, as I have already indicated, there is a general work-based learning literature beyond Education that is concerned with this issue, such as with farmers adopting new crops, doctors introducing new prescribing practices, or women learning about and adopting birth control practices (Valente, 1995). These cases are considered to exemplify a diffusion process based on how individuals influence each other. But in general terms, work-based learning approaches are missing in the Education literature. At the time of writing, there is no adequate theory that explains the process of creating and sharing teacher knowledge, or agreed model for undertaking mentoring and coaching, yet these matters are at the core of the mentoring and coaching debate across professions and industries.

The most productive condition for informal workplace learning is a teacher culture that encourages and values collaborative learning according to Avalos (2012). However, as McCormick (2010) points out, there is a problem with the theoretical basis of CPD literature in general. McCormick (2010) cites Wilson and Berne (1999) to criticise CPD that is based on untested beliefs, such as the importance of teacher 'collaboration', without adequate empirical evidence for these beliefs. (Lawless and Pellegrino 2007) suggest that this is the case.

Although the number of professional development opportunities for teachers has increased, our understanding about what constitutes quality professional development, what teachers learn from it, or its impact on student outcomes has not substantially increased [since 1999].

Opfer and Pedder (2011: p. 376) repeat the criticism that the "process–product logic has dominated the literature on teacher professional learning and that this has limited explanatory ability".

The point is of considerable importance for the following reasons put forward by McCormick (2010). First, the *mechanisms* involving teachers that generate improved student learning need to be demonstrated. Thus, being able to provide evidence that teacher 'collaboration' for example improves student learning does not necessarily then reveal the mechanisms by which such improvement takes place. In the Singapore context, Pak Tee Ng (2012) concludes his study of mentoring and coaching by saying that "there is a paucity of empirical research around mentoring/ coaching, in particular the impact of particular mentoring/ coaching schemes within different contexts and the experiences of the participants in such schemes".

For example, teacher collaboration in professional learning communities (see Stoll et al. 2006 for a review of this literature), are based on a theoretical background of collective learning by teachers 'learning' in a 'community of learners' (Stoll et al. 2006). However, the theoretical model fails to provide evidence for the empirical link *between individual and group learning* (Stoll et al. 2006). McCormick (2010) notes that it is a major problem with the conceptualization of teacher learning.

Second, McCormick (2010) shows that constructs such as 'communities of practice' and 'networks' carry difficult theoretical baggage. In the case of 'communities of practice', the term conceals the fact that when teachers are learning new practices the mentors are rarely 'experts' in that location and situation and, it could be argued, teachers themselves are the 'experts'.

To conceive of, say, those who know how to enact 'learn how to learn' practices in the classroom as a separate 'community of practice', into which other teachers are enculturated, is to create entities that would be hard to identify! (McCormick (2010, 401)

Moreover, the terms 'networks' and 'communities' are often used inter-changeably when they are *different* concepts in social theory. It may not seem like an important issue, but it surfaces repeatedly in the education literature which tends to talk of PD relationships as 'practices' when a sociocultural view sees them as a 'transaction' taking place. The difficulty is that 'practice', says McCormick (2010: p. 404), is "reified by one teacher and conveyed to another, and the other teacher must 'convert' that reification into practice through participation in practice". Thus, 'practices' or 'social transactions' need a substantive theory for understanding the processes that underpin the practices or transactions in social networks, to reveal the underlying conceptualisation that these approaches to 'network' and 'community' entail.

The difficulty occurs both during knowledge 'creation' and 'sharing'. It follows then that to understand how teachers create and share knowledge, it is necessary to have a substantive theory of 'teacher learning' and the mechanisms through which this creation and sharing that leads to 'learning' takes place. Opfler and Pedder (2011, p. 394) reinforce this sentiment in their proposal that ultimately, "we need more studies that investigate how the generative mechanisms of teacher learning appear in different combinations and sequences, with different weights, in different but concrete situations". An important insight here is that the theorisation these authors have in mind goes way beyond views of 'professionalism' and 'professional autonomy' that are the most common forms of Education theorising. It requires systematic work about what happens as a consequence of PD processes.

Moreover, Opfler and Pedder (2011) conclude that there are generalizations about the way professional learning activities relate to teacher learning that are valid *across* different teachers and school contexts. If this is the case then an adequate 'explanatory theory of teacher learning' should be able to distinguish unique, school or teacher dependent aspects of professional learning from those that are generalizable to other teachers and contexts of practice, thus placing prime importance on the conceptualization of PD.

Borko (2004) recognizes the difficulty and attempts to get around the blockages to understanding using a *situative perspective*. This construct refers to physical and social contexts in which an activity takes place as an integral part of the activity; and that the activity is an integral part of the learning that takes place within it. Accordingly, how a person learns a particular set of knowledge and skills, and the situation in which a person learns, become a fundamental part of what is learned. (Putnam and Borko, 2000). Borko (2004) proposes that a situative approach is necessary to explore what she describes as "the most serious unsolved problem for policy and practice in American education today", namely the inadequacy of conventional teacher professional development in everyday life and its theoretical underpinnings. Like Borko, McCormick (2010) cites Little's (1990) work to underline the value of providing a close-grained account of the moral and intellectual dispositions of teachers in their relations with one another, and an account of the actual talk among teachers, the choices they make, and the way in which individual actions follow from the deliberations of the group.

Third, Bausmith and Barry (2011) argue that teacher communities tend to ignore issues related to teaching and learning subject matter even though the research literature has demonstrated the importance of a focus on subject matter learning in programs of teacher professional development (e.g. Fishman, Marx, Best, & Tal, 2003; Kennedy, 1998).

Fourth, in studies of other professions, it has been established that there are influences beyond the collaborating [teacher] group or network. It is worth considering the influences that have an impact on the adoption of new practices in a school, and the extent to which colleagues and friends in other schools or even the Internet might influence teachers.

Fifth, there is repetition in the Education literature about the role of teacher collaboration or mentoring and coaching that are already empirically well established as *effective forms of PD*. Notwithstanding, 'effectiveness' is rarely related to student outcomes (Lawless and Pellegrino, 2007).

'Effectiveness' is a tricky concept in the PD field because of the number of variables involved and the value-loading that it carries in Education, especially in teaching. McCormick (2011) notes that 'effectiveness' could refer to either student or teacher outcomes, and 'experience' can mean a lot of things, as reflected in much of the literature. He proposes the following list as a way of keeping track of the effectiveness of PD.

- There are three targets for impact: *students, teachers* and *school* and a target for each needs to be specified
- Specific reference needs to be made about the *type* of PD such as 'attending external conferences and courses' and the *nature of provision*, for example, 'coaching and mentoring', 'shadowing and peer support', 'lesson observations' and 'discussions with colleagues to reflect on working practices'
- The *direct relevance* of PD to the participants should be specified, with clearly identified *intended outcomes* such as elements of PD activity that are in line with good teaching and learning principles, taking account of previous knowledge and expertise, modelling effective teaching and learning strategies, and impact evaluation

- The *context conditions* for effective PD in the local situation should be identified, to ensure effectiveness. For example, whether or not the culture of the school is conducive to teacher learning.

Opfer and Pedder (2011) suggest that even when changes are detected in teacher behaviour as a result of course work or short-term professional development activities such as more and better field and classroom experiences; opportunities for reflection; opportunities for understanding oneself in a secure environment under challenging or novel circumstances; and applied knowledge about teaching and learning, they may be change *measure artefacts* rather than 'real' changes in teacher orientation. They go to say that:

Despite the close identification of these elements with effective teacher learning and changes in teacher orientation, few … studies empirically connected the specific learning activities to specific changes in teacher belief. Fewer still go further to connect the learning activity to change in learning orientation and change in subsequent teaching practice (Opfer and Pedder, 2011).

Nevertheless, Kim, Egan, Kim and Kim (2013), in a study of direct and indirect effects of managerial coaching behaviour on employee role clarity, work attitudes, and performance, report that managerial coaching behaviour influenced employee role cognition, work attitudes, and performance. They claim that it is one of the first studies to provide evidence for such influence and also point out that there is no commonly acknowledged theory or conceptual model for managerial coaching outcomes. Nor were they able to identify any study of managerial coaching in Asian cultural contexts.

Issue # 3: An Alternative, Indicative Model

Schiemann (2014) provides a different perspective on the same deep issues for transforming an organisation with the concept of 'People Equity', defined as "the collective state of Alignment, Capabilities, and Engagement (or ACE for short)". The People Equity framework was developed in the global business environment but appears eminently adaptable as a coherent model for schools by combining important individual and organisational outcomes, such as quality, productivity, student retention, and organizational processes and policies that drive the optimum use of staff talent. Stoll et al. (2006) also propose that:

> International evidence suggests that educational reform's progress depends on teachers' individual and collective capacity and its link with schoolwide capacity for promoting pupils' learning. Building capacity is therefore critical (Stoll et al., 2006: p. 221).

By 'talent', Schiemann refers to *the collective knowledge, skills, abilities, experiences, values, habits ana behaviours oj ali labour that is brought to bear on the organization's mission.* His concern is to think about "what capability is added to or subtracted from the organization as a result of acquiring or losing a person", the value of talent as a resource where the returns for concentrating on it include benefits beyond financial ones alone. How well talent is leveraged, he argues, provides a competitive advantage a situation well documented in the PISA comparisons and debates about optimum ways for teachers to ply their capacities (PISA.).

Schiemann's (2014) People Equity model, liberally modified for schools, is as follows:

> i. 'Alignment' is the degree to which everyone in the school is rowing synchronously in the same direction. Strong alignment is indicated by behaviours that are aligned with goals, students and the school ethos. Horizontal alignment, units working synchronously together across structural boundaries, is also quite important.

> ii. 'Capabilities' are defined with the major stakeholders in mind. It is the extent to which 'competencies' (e.g. knowledge, skills), information, and resources are sufficient to meet internal or external stakeholder expectations. At the

micro-level, students are the main stakeholders, while at the macro-level, a school is accountable to community and the nation. This focus is especially pertinent in a world where a focus on the students for example slides to a concern about the *providers* of the service (e.g. Policy and Procedures for the Accreditation of Initial Teacher Education Programs in NSW). The importance is underlined by Nuthall (2004: 285) "although there are problems with the assessment of student learning, there is no substitute for going directly to the student when assessing the effectiveness of the teacher". Researchers frequently use student interviews using structured protocols, grades assigned by experienced teachers to various dimensions in portfolios of student work, standardized test scores and multiple forms of assessment simultaneously to increase the richness of evidence and the conclusions that can be drawn from it (Fallon, 2006).

iii. 'Engagement' is comprised of three factors: satisfaction, commitment, and advocacy. The former two factors are central engagement constructs in the teacher or head roles, while advocacy includes extra-role behaviour actions, beyond the minimal requirements of the role. These could include innovative behaviours, extra time in role activities, or going out of the way to recommend the organization to potential employees and students or others. The concept of engagement then includes both the affective states that create the condition for the discretionary effort of satisfaction and commitment and a willingness to take actions on behalf of the organization or others in the organization. For example:

> … when basic satisfaction drivers—job security, compensation and benefits, fairness—dropped in difficult economic conditions, engagement plummeted (Seibert & Schiemann, 2010). In

contrast, when satisfaction and commitment are high, organizations that can also achieve high advocacy—such as endorsing the organization publicly—have the highest engagement (Schiemann, 2014, p. 283).

The pressure on schools to improve student outcomes places stress on individuals who must become *alignea* and *engagea* with the new mission and the culture. The intra-teacher profession about NAPLAN and PISA for instance reveals that there are significant issues for some teachers and their representative organisations to 'fit' with the emergent school goals, values, or culture or there is failure on the part of some individuals to become engaged in the organization. It means that a school has people in place who really don't want to be there and it is the lot of the school leadership to optimize a school's talent by focusing it, developing the right capabilities, and creating engagement (Schiemann, Seibert and Morgan, 2013).

It is important to see the link here with the mentorship literature already cited. It is not just about alignment issues such as polices, procedures and goals or capabilities such as training, but must include engagement aspects to connect leaders to everyone else in the organisation regardless of role and status. Wanting to be part of a team, while being recognized for one's individuality, a welcoming environment, with clear, mutually agreed-upon expectations between teachers and the head and peers foster recognition, growth opportunities, safety and security, fair treatment, and open communication. Such processes ("Onboarding") are crafted early in a new relationship.

Extrapolating from Schiemann (2014), mentoring is an intricate set of behaviours, requiring exceptional skills in evaluating a teacher's performance, correcting deviations from the schools mission etc. and providing feedback, can often compromise engagement. Again, when engagement is muted, motivation to hone skills may drop or increase a person's determination to go elsewhere. Similarly, capabilities can be sacrificed or assumed under pressure to create alignment as leaders focus on goals and gaps without sufficient emphasis on coaching staff so that there is minimal development. As Schiemann (2014) asks, "If a leader doesn't have people who are aligned with the goals and vision, have effective competencies and are engaged in the tasks at hand, isn't something wrong? Is that leader the right person for a job that requires talent optimization?" A summary of Schiemann's model appears in Figure 1.

Nuthall (2004) refers to the 'pragmatic validity' of research. Translating his concept to teacher PD and learning, the issue is how PD is related to teacher learning in a way that is comprehensible and practically useful for the teachers concerned and their school heads (Nutthall, 2004). Nuthall (2004) argues that this approach entails *three distinct but interacting* layers: (a) the visible layer of head-managed activities; (b) the semi-visible layer of teacher-to-teacher culture, relationships, and interactions; and (c) the semi-visible layer of individual teacher behaviours. Drawing on this conceptualisation, the ways teachers behave and consequently experience PD activities are not simply a function of head or coach-managed activities, but also a function of the teachers' ongoing relationships with other teachers and their students and of their own beliefs and previous experiences.

Summing up Nuthall's argument and applying it to teacher PD, the following issues assume high priority.

1. Independent in-depth assessment of what teachers learn. PD effectiveness can only be determined from independent information from individual teachers. Every study must include an assessment of what individual teachers know and can do before and what they know and can do after PD instruction. The assessment needs to be independent of head evaluations. Neither heads nor students are good at evaluating teacher learning (Purser, Knight, & Bedenbaugh, 1990). Observations are preferable, because understanding learning

is not possible unless you understand both the content and complexity of changes in what teachers know and believe.

2. Complete, continuous data on individual teacher experience. Research on PD impact requires direct systematic continuous observation (preferably recording) supplemented with interviews in order to capture, as far as possible, the ways individual teachers experience their PD activities and the content messages embedded in them.

Figure 1: (Schiemann 2014) Alignment, Capability and Engagement[14]

Alignment	Capabilities	Engagement	Profile	
⇧	⇧	⇧	Optimized Talent	
⬇	⬇	⇧	Misguided Enthusiasm	Sub-Optimization
⬇	⇧	⇧	Strategic Disconnect	
⇧	⬇	⇧	Under Equipped	
⇧	⇧	⬇	Disengaged	
⇧	⬇	⬇	Unable/Unwilling	
⬇	⇧	⬇	Wasted Talent	
⬇	⬇	⬇	High Risk	

⇧ High   ⬇ Low

3. Complete, continuous data on PD activities. Recordings of PD activities and teacher experiences must be continuous over the period in which the learning is expected to occur. PD effects are not stable over time and context, and both teaching and learning are continuous, cumulative processes. Recordings and observations need to be focused on individual teachers. Occasional observations or sampled observations do not provide the data needed to connect PD to the teaching process.

---

[14] Taken from Schiemann (2014). Available also at:
http://www.edgef.org/wp-content/uploads/2014/06/Schiemann-slides_Post-Session.pdf

4. Analysis based on the continuous connections among PD activities, teacher experiences, and classroom learning processes. The data must be analysed in a way that sensibly connects the recordings of PD and teacher activities to the process of classroom learning. This means including recordings of the private and hidden social worlds of teachers, as well as the public whole staff environment. It also means a sequentially ordered analysis of the visible structure (Oser & Baeriswyl, 2001) that can be connected in real time to evidence (direct and indirect) of the changes taking place in the minds of the teachers.

5. Avoid the aggregation of data. Aggregation of data across teachers and across different PD outcomes must be carefully justified before it can be used. Individual teachers can have quite different experiences within the same PD, begin with quite different background knowledge, and achieve significantly different outcomes (Nuthall, 1999a). Aggregation by summing introduces unnecessary ambiguity and error, yet generalization across individual cases is the function and substance of theory building, the process discussed elsewhere in this chapter as a prime need in the teacher learning / PD field.

6. Explanatory theory must be directly and transparently connected to relevant evidence. We need to distinguish carefully between speculation and evidence-based theory. Many studies (like those in CPD, PD, teacher learning that lack so much critical intermediary data between the PD activities and individual teacher outcomes) can only produce speculation about the relationship between PD and teacher learning. Usable evidence-based theory needs to be built from the bottom up, from the details of individual teachers and specific PD activities, and requires much more detailed and precise data on what is happening in the PD program and in the minds of teachers.

Of these criteria, the most significant is the second, the need for *continuous observational data on individual teacher experience.* Interpreting and understanding individual behaviour and inferring underlying learning processes depends on knowing the full context in which an individual's behaviour occurs.

Issue # 4: Towards a theoretical synthesis of leadership, effective pedagogy and enhanced student academic outcomes

Heibert et al (2002) propose a challenging approach to moving teaching's knowledge base from researchers' knowledge of teaching to teachers' knowledge. The recent BERA (2014) reinforces this position in its advocacy of teachers as 'researchers'. Against the universally acknowledged background that teachers "rarely draw from a shared knowledge base to improve their practice" and do not "routinely locate and translate research-based knowledge to inform their efforts" (Heibert et al 2002, p. 3), their suggestions are highly relevant to the implementation of mentoring and coaching programs that aim to make an impact on student academic learning outcomes. To that end, their proposals are outlined before moving on.

Heibert et al. (2002) begin by characterising teacher work as examining student work, developing performance assessments and standards-based report cards, jointly planning, teaching, and revising lessons, and exhibiting expertise in lesson presentations. While teachers traditionally have worked in isolation, they report favourably on in-school programs that bring colleagues together in active, collaborative work to improve practice. Nevertheless, as Heibert et al (2002) remind us, an old problem is revealed in a new light as they:

> … rarely search the research archives to help them interpret their students' conceptions and misconceptions, plot their students' learning trajectories, or devise alternative teaching practices that are more effective in helping their students master the curriculum (Heibert et al., 2002, p. 3).

Tomlinson (2008) provides insights here about the obvious dangers of narrow perspectives. Discussing the relationships between psychological theory and pedagogy, Tomlinson identifies "the unfortunate general educator tendency to think in terms just of overt teaching strategies and to ignore the psychological work they must achieve" (Tomlinson; 2008: p. 522-523). He cites Chi & Ohlsson, (2005) to illustrate how a particular teaching strategy (having students self-explain a physics problem) because it forces them to articulate and often repair their mental models, shields the potential to do this by using another teaching strategy (peer tutoring) for the same effect. Again, Tomlinson (2008) refers to selective applications of psychology when for example,

> … a particular subject teaching community develops a relatively exclusive devotion to a particular psychological viewpoint as its 'silver bullet paradigm', as arguably happened with science education's attachment to individual constructivism in the 1980s (e.g. Driver, 1983) (Tomlinson (2008: p. 523).

One might generalise this remark far wider than science education in the Australian Education context and include teacher education and policy development as well.

Returning to Heibert et al. (2002), they refer to teacher's knowledge as "craft" knowledge characterized more by its "concreteness and contextual richness" than its generalizability and context independence. It is linked to practice because it is motivated by the problems of teaching and the fact that each new bit of knowledge is connected to the processes of teaching and learning that actually occur in classrooms. In short, practitioner knowledge is detailed, concrete, specific and integrated and organized around problems of practice. It constitutes a world of its own and it is this characteristic that makes bridging the gap between research knowledge and teachers' practice inherently difficult, if not intractable.

By labelling teacher knowledge in this way is hardly a criticism of its complexity and richness. On the contrary, the description is aimed at unlocking and revealing teacher knowledge to a wider audience than the individual 'gun' teacher or 'gifted' individual, to reveal the fullness of the accumulated wisdom of teaching profession's history.

To unravel the difficulty and intractability of teacher knowledge, Heibert et al. (2002) call on Popper's (1972) three worlds of knowledge, namely World 1, knowledge of physical and real-world objects and experiences; World 2, individuals' knowledge and skills; and World 3, shared ideas treatable as public objects that can be stored and accumulated. Their argument is that teachers interact with their students and the curriculum in World 1, they create knowledge for themselves in World 2, but World 3 is where the teaching profession's knowledge for teaching must be generated. In short:

> ...teachers must operate in a system that allows them to treat ideas for teaching as objects that can be shared and examined publicly, that can be stored and accumulated and passed along to the next generation (Heibert et al., 2002, p. 5ff).

A collaborative environment in schools then becomes the *sine qua non* of professional development in Heibert et al.'s (2002) view, not because collaborations provide teachers with social support groups, but "because collaborations force their participants to make their knowledge public and understood by colleagues". Nonetheless, 'collaboration' alone is insufficient. *Professional knowledge* must also be public, created with the goal of making it shareable among teachers, open for discussion, verification, and refutation or modification. The lack of such qualities in relation to teacher/teaching knowledge is the trademark of an *immature* profession.

To this end, Heibert et al. (2002), take on one of the key elements that make bridging the gap between research knowledge and teachers' practice so difficult: the issue of representing knowledge for teaching through theories offering abstract knowledge that transcends particular classrooms and contexts and ensures that the knowledge rises above idiosyncratic technique with examples. Such theories are in their view, a "hallmark of professional knowledge".

In addition, such theories must offer examples, grounded in practice to reveal the meaning of verbal propositions of theories. This too is a fundamental point about collaborative work. Teachers can readily provide examples of their experiences and practice, but it is not obvious that they can transform their classroom-based knowledge into 'theories' of teaching. Moreover, Heibert et al. (2002) propose, such useful theories are "teacher's hypotheses or predictions regarding the relationships between classroom practices and students' learning, along with explanations for observed connections". Again, it can be readily understood that collaborative work about 'teaching', founded on such principles, meet Bausmith and Barry's (2011) critique that the research on subject matter content and how students learn that content is not typically sought out by teachers.

To facilitate this, and to reduce the complexity of teaching, Heibert et al. (2002) nominate the *lesson* as the most theoretically heuristic and practically accessible unit of analysis and improvement that captures interaction among the features of teaching that give teaching its meaning and character. They also advocate that the quest for theory building about teaching would be enabled by a shared curriculum in contrast to teachers creating their own and pursuing different curriculum goals.

Together, these features create the conditions for teachers or a school to develop and test hypotheses with local theories about the way in which particular lessons facilitate (and undermine) students' learning. Local knowledge as described here is almost always incomplete and 'sometimes blind and insular' invoking concerns about accuracy, verifiability, and continuous improvement. They suggest *storing* such knowledge in a form that can be accessed and used by others, namely video copies of lessons that exemplify hypotheses and local theories. In this way, teachers can continually evaluate theories exemplified in real-world lessons in different contexts to create a quality control mechanism.

Finally, Heibert et al. (2002) are unable to cite a single example in the USA where their prescriptions operate and we would hazard a guess that it is also the case in Australia. They analyse the historical roots of this issue and nominate a Japanese example in which:

> Small groups of teachers meet regularly, once a week for several hours, to collaboratively plan, implement, evaluate, and revise lessons. Many groups focus on only a few lessons over the year with the aim of perfecting these. They begin the process of improving the targeted lessons by setting clear learning goals and then reading about what other teachers have done, what ideas are recommended by researchers and reformers, and what has been reported on students' learning of this topic. Often, they solicit university researchers to serve as consultants to their group. Researchers add perspective to the group's deliberations, bring in the experiences of other groups they have worked with, and help locate research information that refines the group's problems and hypotheses (Heibert et al., 2002, p. 9).

There are echoes of the background to successful PISA results here (Pearson Foundation, 2013).

What the research tells us

Rather than dwelling on the minutiae of the host of articles and books about 'mentoring' and 'coaching' in Education and most other industries, a decision was made to extract what appear to be the dominant ideas of the field, against the projects and activities ongoing in Australian schools and elsewhere. These ideas include the major critiques of existing work and proposals for the future. We conclude this chapter by summarising same into six key themes:

First, 'mentoring' and 'coaching' are core elements of PD or 'teacher learning'. There is work to be done to clarify and make explicit the meaning of 'teacher learning' and its content.

Second, more focused research is needed into what is happening in school PD and the views of teachers and school leaders about those activities. As an illustration of the complexity involved, Hutchinson and Purcell (2007) identified some supportive conditions that promote involvement in and commitment to learning and development in an organisation. Building a 'language of learning and development', to provide a common language for sharing understanding about developmental activities is essential. So too is 'creating a supportive organizational culture' and 'an effective and widely used performance management system'. How these tasks are accomplished and what staff think of them are major research areas.

Third, PD processes need to be theorised more so that a body of principles can be developed that have validity beyond the locale where research evidence is gathered. For Education PD, it is time to distinguish the 'creating' of practices from the 'sharing' of them so that the intricacies can be revealed. Also in Education, it is probably time to transcend the 'community' view of 'teacher networks' unless these troublesome concepts are refined and made more productive. Promising theoretical approaches include 'learning' and there is a range of theories that can be drawn from other disciplines.

Fourth, the role of an outside 'expert' is established in teacher PD, notwithstanding some difficulties with differences of opinion about what expertness means when teachers are learning about pedagogy and curriculum. This point also encompasses the role of published research material that can be accessed and synthesized.

Fifth, teacher PD for whole of school change is a long-term process (e.g. 5 years) involving all school staff and other stakeholders. A planning framework (e.g. alignment, capabilities, engagement) and an expert leadership capacity are mandatory.

Sixth, in all of the teacher learning proposals, there is emphasis on teachers adopting a more 'research-based' approach to their work. This is both a mindset/belief attitude involving investigative skills and capacity to generate, analyse, interpret data and apply research-based findings. It also includes the capability to engage with and synthesize an international research literature about 'learning' and 'instruction' that in 2014 includes web-based resources (see Hirt & Willmott, 2014). How this can happen with the present framing of the 'schoolteacher' role and the nature of the teacher education programs in place and advocated by the accreditation agencies is a vexed question to say the least. On that issue, one might also reference the AITSL (2014) document on professional learning and performance and development that proposes integration, immersion, design-led approaches, market led approaches and open as innovative practices in professional learning and performance and development planning.

5. Coaching, Mentoring and Feedback: The 'How to' in a Schooling Context.

David Lynch and Jake Madden

In this chapter the 'how to' of implementing a coaching, mentoring and feedback regime into a school is outlined. The central premise is based on the orchestration of a coordinated mechanism of 'leadership' and 'data driven decision making' which are then consolidated into a 'coaching, mentoring and feedback' regime for teaching improvement effect.

As earlier chapters have highlighted, Governments across the developed world have begun a focus on improving the educational outcomes of their education systems. Central to their focus is a benchmarking to international comparative studies of student achievement such as the *Programme for International Student Assessment* [PISA] (see OECD, 2013; 2010a; 2010b). Further, an interconnected global economic circumstance, intensified since the emergence of the Knowledge Economy of the 1990s, has created a competitive trade environment dependent upon a highly skilled workforce. This coupling of circumstance has begun to be intensified within schooling systems, with Heads having to develop appropriate plans for the remediation of poor student performance and publicly report on progress. The operational measure of poor performance is an array of standardised and benchmarked tests (predominately in literacy and numeracy) that students undertake each year. In Australia NAPLAN[15] and the 'My School' website are

---

[15] www.naplan.edu.au

examples of this public testing and reporting regime[16]: as is OFSTED in the UK[17] and KHDA[18] in Dubai, UAE. This intensification has become pronounced on the backs of studies by Hattie (2012, 2011, 2009) and Fullan and Hargreaves (2012) which specifically implicate the teaching capacities of individual teachers in such student performance results (Lynch, et al, 2015) and by association, the need for a whole of school remediation strategy (Maughan et al, 2012; Scheerens, 2013; Smith and Lynch, 2010) .

In this chapter we outline the 'how to' of implementing a coaching, mentoring and feedback regime into a school. The central premise is based on the orchestration of a coordinated mechanism of 'leadership' and 'data driven decision making', which are consolidated into a 'coaching, mentoring and feedback' regime for teaching improvement effect. We introduced this mechanism in Chapter 2 as the *Collaborative Teacher Learning Model* (CTLM). What makes the CTLM distinctive is that it comes to represent an insight into what the 'key elements' are that enable a school to improve the teaching capacities of its teachers.

In order to examine the CTLM and to present the central tenets of this chapter we begin by briefly (1) recapping the Collaborative Teacher Learning Model. We then explore (2) coaching, mentoring and feedback; (3) the process that come into play when you implement CMF; (4) the required catalyst for engaging teachers in CFM and (5) a final word. We turn first to a revision of the CTLM for key points of reference.

The Collaborative Teacher Learning Model

As we outlined in Chapter 2 the CTLM is an evidence-based practice scheme coupled to a teaching team-based coaching, mentoring and feedback (CMF) regime. This CMF coupling

---

provides the central mechanism through which the teach**ing** performance of each teacher is assessed and where the strategy for improvement is planned and enacted. Diagram 1 illustrates this arrangement.

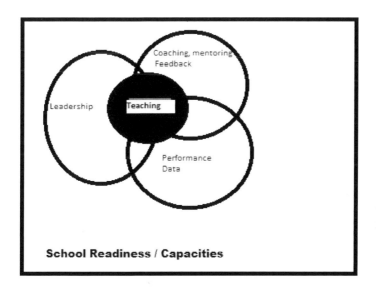

Diagram 1: The Collaborative Teacher Learning Model: key elements

This evidence based mechanism is informed by a school-wide data collection and management system, where timely reports on student progress, using standardised testing results[19] and effect size calculations[20] are provided to each teaching team (evidence regime).

[19] In the case of this study, data was collected about student performance in literacy using standardised tests in spelling, reading, writing language, conventions and writing capacities.

[20] An effect-size provides a common expression of the magnitude of study outcomes for all types of outcome variables, such as school achievement. An effect size of $d = 1.0$ indicates an increase of one standard deviation on student achievement. A one standard deviation increase is typically associated with advancing a student's achievement by *two to three years* or *improving the rate of learning by 50%*. When implementing a new program, an effect size of 1.0 would mean that, on average, students receiving that treatment would exceed 84% of those students not receiving that treatment. Hattie (2012, 2009, 1999), having concluded from an extensive meta study of teaching research, proposed that anything with an effect size of over 0.4 is likely to have a visible, positive effect on student achievement.

This evidence-based regime is further intensified by the use of published peer reviewed education literature, which is referenced by teachers and the school's leaders when making teaching decision. Table 1 in Chapter 2 exemplifies the body of work at the heart of the CTLM.

The leadership of the School's teaching, and thus the embodiment of the CTLM strategy, is consolidated in a series of *teaching team leaders* who in turn are directly supervised by the Head. An interesting observation is that the Head, in the pilot school that perfected the CTLM (See Chapter 2) reconceptualised his role to be the 'chief leader of teaching' and thus the more traditional school administrative tasks (such as internal organisations, finance, facilities, HR and the like) normally assigned to the Head were delegated to other staff. His reference for such a decision was an extensive meta-analysis (study) that Marzano et. al (2005) conducted and which found a 0.25 correlation between a principal's leadership and student achievement. If focused, the Head's leadership could potentially increase student achievement up to 22% higher than the starting percentile (Marzano et al. 2003).

While these aforementioned elements provide an insight into what can be described as the 'visible day to day' elements of the CTLM while in action, it is the elements of 'leadership' and 'school readiness/capacities' which feature prominently, especially in the CTLM's early days, that enabled it to be conceptualised, implemented and refined into the school. We briefly describe and locate each element for reference purposes.

A key innovation in the CTLM is that the scheme extends the leadership functions of the school to a designated 'expert teacher' in each teaching team. This is a contrast to the traditional school establishment structure where the Head and his deputy (or faculty heads) oversee the work of the school, but chiefly from an administrative and organisational perspective: meaning not exclusively to 'teaching'. The 'expert teacher' facilitates the enacting of the CTLM and its associated elements for <u>teaching improvement</u> effect *in* their teaching team. In the context of the pilot school these teams were constituted around a year or grade level (ie: all Year 1 teachers, n=4, students n=100). The use of an 'expert teacher' is important in the CTLM because this teacher's demonstrated expert level teaching capacities --- in other words the performance data for this teacher, on the various metrics used, indicates that they have acquired a high capacity to achieve sustained learning outcomes in their students --- is pivotal to building the required teaching capacities of the less able teaching team members. While they were deemed 'experts' they were called 'teaching team leaders' in the pilot school.

The final element to explain is the 'schools readiness/capacities'. In simple terms this comes to represent a series of considerations and capacities that enable the school as a whole to develop, implement, sustain and review the CTLM. These considerations and capacities includes things such as an analysis of significant organisational challenges; the required communication mechanism within the school, a budget, etc, and of course an articulated and agreed school improvement vision (Fullan and Hargreaves, 2012; Maughan, et al, 2012; Fullan, 2006; Darling-Hammond, 1997) as well as identifying the required first order and second order leadership arrangements (Marzano, et al, 2005).

To this point the CTLM has been outlined from a key elements perspective. However, the engine room, as it were in the CTLM, is a regime of coaching, mentoring and feedback facilitated by the 'expert teacher' in each teaching team. In the third part of the chapter the mechanics of coaching, mentoring and feedback are discussed and elaborated upon.

Coaching, Mentoring and Feedback (CMF)

As we detailed in Chapter 4, Mentoring has ancient origins, but modern day mentoring has roots in the European apprenticeship system, when the apprentice learnt skills from the master craftsman (Clutterbuck, 1985). This legacy leads to many images of 'mentoring' that reflect the difficulty of exact definition (see Carter, 2013; DfES, 2005). While coaching in an organizational sense has traditionally been viewed as a way to correct poor performance and to link individual effectiveness with organizational performance (Ellinger et al., 2003), the distinction between coaching and mentoring has not been clear.

Organizations and the literature use the terms mentoring and coaching interchangeably. More specifically, coaching and formal mentoring are similar in nature but different in name (Joo, Sushko & McLean, 2012 p. 30). We follow this advice except where either mentoring or coaching is the core of the discussion. In addition, the construct teacher 'Professional Development' (PD) can be rendered as 'Continuing Professional Development' (CPD), teacher learning, school improvement and so on. In each of them, we argue that mentoring and coaching play a key role in their implementation. For references purposes, the DfES (2005) statement provides the following definitions for an education context:

- "Mentoring is a structured, sustained process for supporting professional learners through significant career transitions;

- Specialist Coaching is a structured, sustained process for enabling the development of a specific aspect of a professional learner's practice;

- Collaborative (Co-) Coaching is a structured, sustained process between two or more professional learners to enable them to embed new knowledge and skills from specialist sources in day-to-day practice."

Hamlin et al. (2006, p. 326) conclude, "Truly effective managers and managerial leaders are those who embed effective coaching into the heart of their management practice". Cordingly and Buckler (2012, 221) make the point that for those studies showing a "positive impact on both teacher and learner outcomes" of mentoring and coaching, the most important messages are the processes involved: collaboration, sustained, embedded in real-life learning contexts, and supported by specialists. Moreover, in order to enable these things, school leaders need to focus much of their effort on the core business of teaching and learning (Robinson, Hohepa & Lloyd, 2010) so that teaching leaders and teachers in the school also have a heightened awareness of the importance of inquiring into the impact of their teaching on student academic outcomes.

The key point is that when teachers develop their own inquiry skills and can apply them, it is more likely that there will be sustained improvement in teaching effectiveness (BERA, 2013; Timperley, Wilson, Barrar & Fung 2009). This is a key point that needs consideration in implementing the CTLM as a later section affirms. Thus, as MacBeath and Dempster (2009) point out, the teaching role is delineated as delivering a curriculum, but with systematic inquiry into curriculum and the art and science of teaching. For contemporary teachers, these concepts constitute professional knowledge, and leadership that leads to a successful amalgam of these at the teacher level is all about capacity building (Smith & Lynch, 2010): the goal of coaching and mentoring in the CTLM. Mentoring and coaching, are fundamental in school settings where professional development is inextricably linked with the personal history of the individual teachers involved. Let us elaborate.

Each teacher has a personal angle on 'teaching' and teaching style, determined by accumulated knowledge and ideas, perceptions of the profession, and era in which they undertook teacher education (Lynch & Smith, 2012; Kozloff, 2005). Bringing this enormous array of differences and similarities to the table for disciplined dialogue is a priority for school leaders where the psychosocial functions present special challenges. In more simple terms a whole of school improvement strategy requires *all* teachers to be 'aligned' in their understanding of and their capacity for competent teaching: to be on the same page as it were (Schiemann, 2012, 2009b).

Nevertheless, the mentoring role is fraught not just for school leaders. Spaten and Flensborg's (2013) study of 15 middle managers trained to coach 75 employees found that the manager as coach has to be sensitive and empathetic in building the coaching relationship and should draw clear boundaries between their role as leader with a power relationship and supportive coach. Seibert (2013) in a study of 11 companies and 5,000 employees reports that where employees believed that their managers provided ongoing coaching and feedback to help them succeed, 93% reported a willingness to put in additional effort when needed, compared to only 33% of those who reported poor coaching and feedback. If this study is representative, it suggests that mentoring and coaching skills are a core capability for leaders and that even then, the processes can go wrong.

In the pilot school the 'expert teacher' in each team was co-opted as the 'teaching team leader' through the implementation of a new school leadership structure that focused on building teacher capacity through team-based coaching and mentoring. This small team arrangement was deliberate in that it set about firstly to humanise the process and thus make each member feel at ease, and secondly was presented to members as a teaching capacity strategy. It's direct link to each teacher's work --- a year or discipline level team --- had the additional effect of ensuring a focus on the core business of 'teaching' in the team. It was not sold to teachers as a strategy to identify poor performing staff, but as a means by which the teaching capacities of each teacher would be strengthened and the collective capacities of the team harnessed to deal with the multitude of challenges individual students posed: the mantra for teachers was "a problem shared is a problem halved"[21]. For the pilot school's Head, his mantra was enmeshed in a realisation that his school would only ever be as good as the sum of all of his teachers' teaching capacities. Hence the focus on every teacher's teaching.

The third arm to the pilot school's coaching and mentoring schema is the premise of 'feedback'. Feedback is intrinsically intertwined in the process of coaching and mentoring in that it is information about how well one is doing in their efforts to achieve a goal is revealed. Or as Hattie and Timperley (2007, p.81) state,

> "…feedback is conceptualized as information provided by an agent (e.g., teacher, peer, book, parent, self, experience) regarding aspects of one's performance or understanding. A teacher or parent can provide corrective information, a peer can provide an alternative strategy, a book can provide information to clarify ideas, a parent can provide encouragement, and a learner can look up the answer to evaluate the correctness of a response. **Feedback thus is a 'consequence' of performance.** (Bold added)

In the CTLM, feedback was incorporated into the coaching/ mentoring process by way of regular reports on student learning performance coupled to teaching observation reports, both oral and written (a template was used to focus the observer). These were also coalesced into a periodic report referenced and benchmarked to agreed performance

---

[21] http://www.usingenglish.com/reference/idioms/a+problem+shared+is+a+problem+halved.html

goals and targets[22]. We hasten to add that feedback in the CTLM was not an end point, but an ongoing catalyst for teaching improvement. The process of feedback creates the required dialogue and the desire in the teacher (the mentee) and their coach/mentor (expert teacher) to decide what to focus upon next, while the agreed targets and goals provided the base from which to judge how well same is being achieved. Goals and targets in the CTLM were expressly student-learning outcomes referenced, but included a series of other 'teacher' specific elements (from specific teaching skills to discipline knowledge and understanding) in a quest for the teacher to improve their teaching practice. The dynamics of the teaching team is also used to support the implications of such feedback. To this extent feedback, like the processes of coaching and mentoring, are framed in a sequential process of planning, organisation, instruction and leadership: or what is termed in the CTLM as 'POIL'. POIL comes to represent the framework for recruiting and then aligning teachers into the process of coaching, mentoring and feedback.

The Process of Coaching and Mentoring: POIL

The challenge in a school reform process that seeks to impact the teaching capacities of teachers is 'the how to' strategy. As experienced principals will tell you, a well organised and functional school --- meaning everyone appearing to go about 'their business' with a sense of cohesive style and purpose and which is on display for everyone to see --- is perhaps the long established layman's yardstick for judging the well-run school. To jeopardise this perception is to unleash all manner of career limiting calamity for the Head, let alone unsettle any relative calm

---

[22] A designated administrative officer was charged with preparing required reports for teams and the school's leadership

within the perpetually busy modern school (Lynch, 2012; Madden, 2012). Aside from all this it once again highlights the importance of competent leadership in projects such as the CTLM. While our comments might be viewed as a cynical excuse for a Head not wanting to reform their school, the real impediment appears to reside in a long established school design feature that renders each teacher working in isolation from their teaching peers and supervisors: the single teacher, closed door classroom configuration (Lynch, 2012; Abbott, 1999).

At its heart the enacting of a coaching, mentoring and feedback regime aims to 'de-privatise teaching'[23] such that it seeks to disrupt the premise of teachers working on their own and behind closed doors: without necessarily removing physical walls (Madden, 2012). CMF in effect projects the work of the single teacher into a teaching team arrangement such that what the teacher does and the outcomes of same become visible to others. This is done by way of teachers [1] working collaboratively when planning and then contributing to the delivery of the curriculum for *the whole* cohort of students[24] --- i.e. not just a concern with their own assigned cohort --- [2] having their practice regularly reviewed by members of their teaching team; [3] and a plan for their resulting professional development consolidated into a process of coaching and mentoring by their assigned 'team leader'. [4] Overall 'Performance' in this arrangement is enmeshed in 'feedback', which is referenced to agreed goals and targets which in turn is referenced to student performance data and observational teaching skill metrics and indicators.[25]

---

[23] http://www.interlead.co.nz/interlead-programmes/enhancing-student-achievement-by-de-privatising-practice-and-de-privatising-classrooms/

[24] In the context of the CTLM pilot project a teaching team cohort comprised all the teachers in a Year level. e.g: Year 3. In secondary schools this might, for example include all faculty staff in science.

Interestingly, in the pilot school (as detailed and examined in Chapter 2), peer pressure became a key motivating factor for the 'reluctant to change teacher', in that the process of feedback tended to implicate the teaching capacity of the overall team, not unlike how one flat tyre affects the whole car's performance.

To enable the coaching, mentoring and feedback regime to have a sense of body and process teams use what we term the *POIL* framework. The point we wish to emphasise is that in effect teacher engagement with each 'frame' of POIL presents a sequential opportunity for the 'team leader' to coach and mentor members of their team (and/or for other team members to be co-opted to also act as coach and mentor. The determining factor is always the competency level of the coach/ mentor).

The 'POIL' framework is built upon an acronym from *Planning, Organisation, Instruction and Leadership*. Each 'frame' comes to represent a sequential set of key elements that the team leader, and by direct association, the assigned teaching team, have to consider together in their quest to improve their overall teaching performance. We briefly elaborate each element.

Planning Frame

In the traditional single classroom teaching arrangement, the teacher is assigned a teaching cohort (25 to 30 students), generally a 'share' of a year level or discipline area in the school and which is perceived as being 'fair' in terms of student abilities and numbers (ie: the industrially based 'equal' workload allocation). Then, using the appropriate school planning documents, the teacher, on their own, plans

---

[25] In the context of the CTLM pilot school teaching skills were judged using the Australian Professional Standards for Teachers. Located at http://www.aitsl.edu.au/australian-professional-standards-for-teachers

a program of instruction. Limited teaching capacity in the classroom (ie: just themselves) generally inclines the teacher to teach strictly to the scope of their year/discipline level curriculum and where possible utilise a teacher's aide and extension/remediation programs (ie: paper based resource books) to deal with those students who don't fit age appropriate learning norms. While the curriculum attempts to represent a manageable level of content 'to be covered' (in a term/school year) the reality of student learning performance, in any given classroom, can be one of extremes (Hattie, 2009) and thus the teacher's ability to adequately deal with each individual student's learning needs in such arrangements is somewhat diminished (Madden, 2012). Couple these circumstances to an 'isolated' teacher, where feedback mechanisms are often self-serving (without third party input) and you have very limited scope for teaching improvement.

In the planning frame all teachers in the teaching team (eg: all Year 3 teachers) meet and discuss the profile of **each** student. In effect they open their classrooms up for coaching, mentoring and feedback. Where student performance data is limited or incomplete the team enacts appropriate assessments (standardised and norm referenced and/or diagnostic) or petitions the Head to acquire more detailed performance results or access to specialist interpretations. A base-line set of data becomes important for gauging learning growth. Teachers then collaboratively plan a course of instruction, where the collective teaching capacities of the team are harnessed to best effect for *all* students. In the pilot school this had the effect of teachers streaming students into custom arrangements dependent on student profiles and need, thus teachers were able to deal with students more efficiently and as pilot study data suggests, more effectively. The use of a teaching design organiser such as the *Learning Management Design Process* (Lynch and Smith, 2012 see also Chapter 8) with its '8 key planning questions' proves an effective tool in such a process. The 8 questions, and which can be used to facilitate the Planning phase are:

Q1: What have our students achieved to date?
- A Global Student Performance profile: *Review performance data*

Q2: What do we aim to achieve in our students?
- Outcomes set based on profiles (together with targets and goals for instructional outcomes)

Q3: How do our students best learn?
- Reviewing the literature for evidence based best practice
- Considering the peculiarities of the cohort

Q4: What resources do we have at our disposal?
- The means to enact plans

Q5: What are our teaching strategies?
- The Application of Evidence Based Strategies to achieve the defined learning outcomes

Q6: Who will do what to achieve support our teaching strategy?
- The team arrangements harnessed for effect

Q7: How will we check that students have achieved the defined learning outcome?
- The assessment and data collection strategy

Q8: How will we report student progress?
- Reporting
- Identifying gaps in the data profile for the next planning phase.

From a coaching and mentoring point of view, the team leader leads the process and in doing so is focused on building the *planning* capacities of each teacher. In a cyclic process subsequent feedback mechanisms will require teachers to revisit the planning frame to take corrective action and thus further coaching and mentoring is embedded through this frame.

By the end of the planning frame, each teacher will have become 'signatory' to a set of teaching plans for the global cohort of students (in a year level, discipline area) and thus their teaching role within is defined. In effect each teacher has agreed on a set of performance goals and targets to be met. The planning frame will be complete when plans have been expanded to make it 'teaching ready' by each teacher.

In summary, the team leader will have engaged teachers in interrogating available and appropriate learning performance data and then coached and mentored teachers in making appropriate and corresponding teaching planning decisions. This frame is enacted first as 'whole of team' and then into 'one-on-one' sessions with less competent teachers. The process of feedback, referenced to subsequent student performance data, will inform the next planning iteration and by association the teacher's subsequent coaching/mentoring focus with their 'team leader'.

Organisation Frame

The organisational frame in effect engages the individual teacher to thinking through the 'organisation' of the teaching plan. The logic is that a collaborative teaching plan has been developed *–planning frame–-* and it then becomes incumbent upon each teacher to 'organise' his or her classroom for implementation. From a coaching and mentoring point of view the organisational frame enables the team leader to enter the classroom --- to break the ice for actual teaching observations (in the next frame) --- and to appraise themselves of the organisational viability. Considerations include; seating arrangements; the use of the classroom and its environs; the day to day management of the classroom and its students, inclusive of the protocols that enable a classroom to be functional and effective as a place of teaching and learning: as well as the classroom culture and climate that has to be developed/evident (Marzano, et al, 2001). The organisational frame can also be extended to include those peripheral, yet important teacher tasks, such as conducting parent-teacher interviews, disciplining students and coordinating support staff. In effect a sound organisational arrangement becomes the second tier in a foundation for effective instruction. Learning Design Questions 3, 4 and 6 are helpful in planning such key organisational elements.

Instruction Frame

The third stage in the POIL framework is a focus on instruction. In this frame a series of classroom visits are made during the course of instruction (i.e. the scope of plans made in the 'planning frame'). These 'visits' are chiefly made by the team leader, however through organisational arrangements in the pilot school, co-opted members of the teaching team would often join the team leader to add to the 'team effect'. These visits take on a number of rather fluid approaches, each determined by the 'improvement need' of the mentee teacher: a body of knowledge known as 'Learning Walks' exemplifies the process[26]:

a) Formal teaching observations using a checklist of teaching capacities/ capabilities[27]

---

[26] https://www.eduweb.vic.gov.au/edulibrary/public/region/loddonmallee/lt-litlearningwalks.pdf

b) Demonstration lessons by the 'expert teacher' of a key competency/ capability

c) Collaborative teaching tasks with the 'expert teacher' (or other teachers) acting as lead teacher with the mentee assisting/ co-teaching

d) Role plays and enactments to hone specific skills and approaches

Generally the process commences with a 'pre-meeting' of the team leader and the mentee where specific performance data, in conjunction with agreed targets and goals are reviewed such that an agreed purpose for the visit is established. Notes are taken for record purposes. Subsequent to this visit a 'post meeting' takes place and what was observed and experienced is formatively discussed. In a cyclic process the premise of another visit is thus planned and the process continues. We hasten to add that the focus is upon the mentee being coached and mentored into improved teaching and the process is such that these 'visits' become normalised as part of working as a teacher in the school.

Leadership Frame

The premise of the overall CTLM is the growth of each and every teacher in the school. To this end the last frame is that of leadership. While this frame can be viewed as a strategy to create future school leaders, the strategy is chiefly designed to enable each teacher to engage with others as a leader in areas where they have expertise. In effect the professional growth of teachers is expanded in this frame such that the school becomes a coordinated entity of competent teachers each with a role to play and the capacities to capitalise on same for overall effect. Teaching teams evolve in time from reliance on

---

[27] Use was made of the Australian Institute for Teaching and School Leadership proformas. See http://www.aitsl.edu.au/classroom-practice

the team leader as 'expert' to everyone having key roles to play in their team and thus having the leadership capacities to perform as required. The Australian Professional Standards for Principals provides guidance in this matter.[28]

A Catalyst for Engaging Teachers in CFM

To this point in the chapter we have outlined the *Collaborative Teacher Learning Model* (CTLM) and in doing so have explained how its central tenets (leadership, school readiness capacities, CFM and performance data) are all focused to 'teaching' improvement. The key mechanism or 'engine room' in the CTLM is a regime of coaching, mentoring and feedback that is established into 'teaching teams' and facilitated by the team leader. The process, which embodies this CMF regime is outlined through four sequentially, enacted lenses known as *POIL: planning—organisation—instruction—leadership.* Taken together these elements provide a theoretical framework through which the Head can enact teaching improvement in their school. But research into the pilot school revealed that a chasm existed between the theoretical processes of the CTLM, irrespective of the research evidence to support it, and the teachers' collective willingness to engage meaningfully with it.

In this section of the chapter we provide a brief insight into a catalyst that was used in the pilot school to enable teachers to 'position' and 'locate' the benefits of the CTLM into their own teaching roles. In more simple terms, it became apparent in the pilot school that when the CTLM was introduced to teachers and their teaching teams, teachers found it difficult to see how it all meshed with their 'teaching world' (BERA, 2013; Maughan, et al, 2012; Hargreaves and Fullan, 2012; Timperley, Wilson, Barrar & Fung 2009). While the

---

[28] http://www.aitsl.edu.au/australian-professional-standard-for-principals

performance data was especially tagged and explained in terms of their teaching cohort and various proformas and templates designed to scaffold teaching decisions, the reality was that teachers did not have ownership of what they considered were 'third party' material. Further when it came time to begin the process of CMF, and its implementation through POIL, teachers reported the agenda as being too large to comprehend and thus needed further refinement and focus. To these ends teachers developed a 'performance task' and it thus became the catalyst for teachers to engage in the CMF part of the CTLM. Diagram 2 illustrates this task in the context of the CTLM.

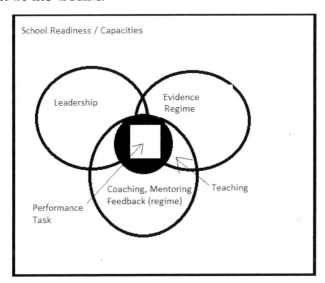

Diagram 2: CTLM and a Performance Task

You will recall, in the context of the pilot school, that English performance was the focal area for improvement. To this end teachers developed a 'writing task' and an associated marking rubric for their teaching team based student cohort. In later iterations the rubric and task were standardised across the school and was referenced to the NAPLAN rubrics[29] to

---

[29] See http://www.nap.edu.au/verve/_resources/2012_marking_guide.pdf

create more validity. The rubric was coded with scores to enable statistical calculations and performance reports to be provided/ compared. Teachers were provided with skilling to make and interpret these calculations at the team level, however it became apparent in the pilot school over time that this was best done at the central school office level.

The writing task was administered pre and post a teaching planning cycle, but importantly for teachers was used not only as a diagnostic tool but also a teaching tool. In the pilot school teaching teams started with a focus on 'narrative writing'[30], and in reference to the school's English curriculum, developed a task that reflected the scope of commensurate writing skills in each year or discipline level. These became the goals for their students in the cohort. The deficit in performance that emerged was then used to scaffold and guide teaching planning and subsequent organisations in the team. Further, these resulting plans then informed the key mechanism of coaching, mentoring and feedback, through the POIL process.

In summary teachers were able to develop their own teaching instrument and thus gained a sense of ownership and territory in the CTLM. This 'instrument' importantly provided them with diagnostic as well as teaching guidance and structure, which they then used to focus their planning and which became the focal points in the coaching, mentoring and feedback regime through POIL.

A Final Word

We make the comment that as the pressures to improve teaching and student outcomes increase, school heads are daily faced with issues such as how teachers and their middle managers can be most effective at work and how

---

[30] See http://www.nap.edu.au/naplan/writing/writing.html

their commitment to common goals determined both beyond the school and within can be encouraged and sustained. To participate in disciplined dialogue, coaching, mentoring and feedback (CMF) becomes an essential technique in schools as it offers an approach to both the work place individual and the personal side of human development in so far as individuals can be helped to explore their potential. Hence, CMF is about an individual's relationship to their work and their ability to thrive within it. The humanising approach that coaching and mentoring engenders, perhaps when stripped of any imposing terminology that may threaten the sensibilities of educators, offers a resource to perceptive education leaders. The incorporation of CTLM as the overarching organiser and CMF implementation frames such as POIL provide a level of guidance that enables each required aspect or foundation for teaching improvement to be considered for effect.

Taken together what this chapter seeks to illustrate are the following key points:

1. **In any change process leadership is important.** As an earlier section detailed the 'pilot school' was what can be described as a 'seed' school. These schools have a strong capacity for change, where the staff is cohesive and excited about teaching. The staff profile in the pilot school did not just emerge it was the product of the school's leader. In a strategic teaching improvement process, leadership capacity in the school was expanded to team leaders who conducted a similar role, but at an intimate level. This is important in the CMF regime. We hasten to add though that without the Head's staunch commitment and drive to improve the pilot school, the results of the pilot school would not have been as positive.

2. There are mountains of information currently available to schools: each seeking to define what good teaching is and

how it can be achieved. The **Collaborative Teacher Learning Model (CTLM) consolidates this mountain into a series of organisational signposts, making the strategic considerations** --- the evidence pathway --- for such a project much clearer for the Head and others.

3. The thesis of this chapter is one that reaffirms the fundamental role that teachers play in achieving learning outcomes in students. Correspondingly **the competence of teachers to teach is commensurate to their professional growth and development.** To this end the process of coaching, mentoring and feedback (CMF) becomes a normalised process within a school such that teachers are engaged in a continual process of improvement. In more simple terms, to remain a competent teacher is to involve oneself in a process of CMF.

4. The premise of **POIL (planning, organisation, instruction, leadership) provides a level of guidance as to what needs to be impacted if CMF** is to have traction with teachers and lead importantly to student learning improvements. To this end the application of these four frames provides a path on which teaching is continually improved for student learning effect.

5. **Teachers having ownership of the 'team-based' strategy** in the CTLM agenda through a catalyst ---'student-based assessment /planning/ teaching/ task'--- is a consideration, especially in early days, when Heads are wanting to enable teachers to 'come on board' and thus position and locate the benefits of same into their teaching role.

6. Making Teacher Professional Learning Effective

Tina Doe

Engaging staff in professional development is an important aspect of creating the outstanding school. The challenge is finding a model that focuses endeavours so they have the required effect. The *Teacher Professional Learning Initiative* (TPLI) is presented in this chapter as an example of a model that focuses on creating outstanding teachers through a particular type of learning partnership.

Introduction

Teachers leaving the school to attend 'face to face' professional development 'workshops' is the norm in the professional life of a teacher. One-off sessions are attended and which effectively represent a compliance issue having been 'ticked off'. As far as engaging, growing and sustaining the teacher professionally most fall well short (Lynch, 2012; Hardwell, 2003). As previous chapters have outlined, teacher learning is a key strategy in the outstanding school agenda. So how might 'PD' be conceptualized to be more effective?

In this chapter the *Teacher Professional Learning Initiative* (TPLI) is presented as an approach to teacher professional learning. While the *Collaborative Teacher Learning Model* of Chapters 2 and 5 came to represent a 'whole of school model and associated strategy, with component pieces organized for teaching improvement', the TPLI is a related part in that it focuses to a key aspect, 'teacher learning'.

The TPLI has been conceptualised as a 'fit for purpose' teaching enhancement model that is tailored to the professional learning needs of each teacher in a school. In order to explain the TPLI I first locate the initiative in the context of a changed world. Next, the four-stage TPLI model is described and the implementation guidelines associated with it elaborated. Finally I provide summary research findings into the TPLI, to highlight the initiatives efficacy. I turn first to the premise of a changed world.

A Changed World

As previous chapters have outlined, the Knowledge Economy that is the current reality for 21st Century educators is a circumstance that has transformed the focus of the previous industrial era to one based on knowledge, as opposed to raw materials. In this new world order knowledge and one's capacity to use it in new and interconnected ways is disrupting all aspects of society. Mechanization and automation coupled with miniaturization and connectivity are extinguishing many labour based jobs, creating many new jobs, but importantly these jobs require increasing levels of education for incumbents. In summary, the Knowledge Economy coupled with the exponential use of social media as communication, represent a fast paced set of ongoing changes in all sections and stratas of society. Given the role that schools play in preparing young people for life and work in such a changed society, pressure has been mounting on schools and teachers to rethink what they do.

This pressure has intensified in recent years because a changed world based on technological innovation has also resulted in greater understandings about how people learn and consequently what the high-yield practices (Marzano et al., 2007; Marzano et al., 2001; Marzano et al. 1999) are to enhance teaching. Further to this, is the increased public press awarded to and consequent increased community interest in the results of international testing regimes such as PISA and ISA[31]. The result is there is data that indicates

---

[31] [31]See http://www.oecd.org/pisa/ and http://www.acer.edu.au/isa

deficits in teaching performance (Caldwell, 2006; MACER, 2004; Department of Education, Science and Training (DEST), 2001) and there is research about how to enhance teacher practice (Fullan, 2011; Hattie, 2009 & 2003). The TPLI has been specifically designed to skill teachers for this new professional context (Doe, 2011) by putting the research about teacher professional learning into practice to improve teaching.

Having made these brief introductory comments, I now turn to a detailing of the Teacher Professional Learning Initiative.

Teacher Professional Learning Initiative (TPLI)

As I briefly outlined in an earlier section, the TPLI is a school-based teaching enhancement model designed to focus teachers in a school to improving their teaching practice. The TPLI is fundamentally built upon three pillars. These three pillars were formulated through a Literature Review, which drew primarily from the work of Darling-Hammond, Fullan, Hattie, Lynch and Marzano. The three pillars are:

1. The TPLI aims to enhance teacher practice through
   - ➤ the use of action learning;
   - ➤ planned and continuous professional learning;
   - ➤ a common language; and
   - ➤ professional learning communities
2. Nine key components constitute the TPLI
3. Teacher participants are 'ready' to engage in professional learning through a TPLI.

On a more specific level, the TPLI is established in a school through three domains: the organisational, the personal, and the technical (McREL, 2000). By domains I mean centres in which impact or change occurs. These three domains are thus 'centres of focus' in the TPLI where a series of 'four stages' are introduced to enact the TPLI. These four stages comprise steps and processes, while stringently referenced to established research (Darling-Hammond (2010 & 2000); Fullan (2011); Hattie (2009 & 2003) & Marzano et al., (2007, 2001 & 1997) and subsequent research conducted into the TPLI (Doe 2015, 2014, 2013, 2011, 2006; Doe et al., 2006) are elaborated for effect by a set of implementation guidelines. These four stages are detailed in Figure 1.

It is important to mention that these four stages are not defined by specific time frames, as the amount of time spent to accomplish each stage is dependent upon the context, the readiness of staff to progress to the next stage and the overall extent of focus placed upon professional learning in the school. The latter is a realisation that the TPLI requires commitment and thus prioritising in the professional learning life of the school. My key point is that each sequential stage creates a roadmap for engaging with the TPLI and thus time comes to represent a key aspect of the customisation and fit to each schooling context.

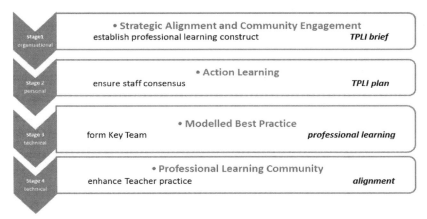

Figure 1: The TPLI Framework (tinadoe.com © 2013)

TPLI Implementation

The TPLI framework above has resulted from my experience in implementing the TPLI in more than 250 schools over 10 years. While the TPLI must be considered as a cohesive and inter-related process using the linear format outlined in Figure 1, it is conceptualised, planned and then implemented at each school as a purpose-fit to identified needs. To this end Figure 1 really comes to represent an 'implementation framework' which has associated steps within that may have to be revisited at varying junctures as the initiative is rolled out. My point here is that by its very nature any system or process is made up of parts, or in this case, 'stages', and the teaching interactions that occur within and as a result of engagement with each stage are what create teaching improvement effect across the system of participant schools. Figure 1 is thus a framework for implementing the TPLI.

I briefly discuss each stage for points of reference.

Strategic Alignment and Community Engagement

Stage 1 of the TPLI framework attends to the organisational domain (McREL, 2000), the product of this stage is a TPLI brief which establishes a through-line, a clear articulation of how the professional learning initiative will backward map from the intended impact evidence to the stated learning intention. Crucial to this stage is that the Instructional Leadership Team make space for the initiative by ensuring that the professional learning has initiated in response to deliverables and identified strategic needs. The professional learning construct is thus established through quality assured processes that target data sets to inform practice, specifically using the school's common pedagogical language. Stage 1, Strategic Alignment and Community Engagement, is about making space for the TPLI and requires that senior executive team demonstrate purposeful visibility and that staff agree to work in Expert Teams, focused to particular goals, to achieve shared vision.

Action Learning

Stage 2 of the TPLI framework, Action Learning is a consideration of the personal domain (McREL, 2000) and in this stage the TPLI professional learning plan is formalised and developed in consultation with Expert Teams of staff who engage in any number of action research projects specific to the TPLI focus that test practices for efficacy. Action Learning is a professional learning model described by Hogan (2001) and was deemed most appropriate to underpin a TPLI. Action learning is designed to focus on teacher pedagogy, as it is relevant to the profession, market needs and public opinion in a global knowledge society. Hogan stipulates that enrolment in an action learning professional learning program should be voluntary, with each person deciding that the problem to be addressed matters, and judging that the method, however vaguely grasped at the initial stage, is likely to result in improvement. He notes that school-based action learning projects are usually built around a problem, issue, opportunity or initiative of concern to the school and/or the wider professional community.

The work of the action learning group or in the context of a TPLI, Expert Team, becomes a project developed within the overall priorities of the school or network and conceptualised through Hogan's eight key components: objectives, timeframes, resources, plans, strategies, support, maintenance and evaluation. Stage 2 is about Instructional Leaders taking time to consider how to engage Expert Team members in action learning through research and reflection of their practice in a collaborative culture (Doe, 2015).

Modelled Best Practice

Stage 3, Modelled Best Practice considers the McREL (2000) technical domain by addressing how teachers will find a place in their repertoire of practice to adopt and adapt the high yield practices that have been tested in the Stage 2, Action Learning. In this stage a Key Team of Instructional Leaders, drawn from all of the Expert Teams, share their findings, prioritise improvement strategies and plan professional learning that will align curriculum, pedagogy and assessment through a shared framework for teaching and learning. Stage 3 Modelled Best Practice is about ensuring that there is a sustainable professional learning program, facilitated by a range of Expert Team members that is planned and continuous and engages staff so that they place their new skills and knowledge by embedding in immediate practice.

Professional Learning Comunity

In a TPLI, a learning community is formed by a group of people, whose common purpose generates collaborative and productive sharing (Doe, 2011) in order to develop new knowledge of mutual benefit (Bloomfield, 2009). Learning communities create a sustainable context, where ongoing and continuous professional learning develops in response to concurrent partner needs (BECTA, 2008; Hennessey & Deaney, 2004 & 2007). Learning communities that are networked (Darling-Hammond, 2010; Zeichner, 2010) are deemed to be more sustainable.

Stage 4 again considers the technical domain (McREL, 2000), specifically how to pace professional learning so that it meets differential needs of the Professional Learning Community. This stage is demonstrated when reciprocal accountability is achieved (Elmore, 2011). Elmore (2011) describes the synergous nature required for an efficacious TPLI as reciprocal accountability – where capacity is created to meet every expectation of performance increment and for every professional learning investment made there is a reciprocal responsibility to demonstrate evidence in practice.

At its very heart the TPLI is designed to engage Instructional Leaders to create capacity for their teachers to demonstrate pedagogical capability at the relevant standard. A TPLI is a networking mechanism that engages teachers in school-wide discourse about professional practice, strategic development and improvement plans and associated specific professional learning activities that positively impact each teacher's teaching capacity. In effect teachers, in a school that is implementing the TPLI, are enmeshed in a constant state of designed professional learning where various feedback loops focus them to the 'next steps'. This four stage framework is currently being used in a number of Australian schools to focus on teaching improvement and the extent of improvement is being measured by relative gains in student learning using standardised testing regimes such as NAPLAN and state-wide assessment and moderation processes.

At its fundamental level the TPLI comes to represent a theoretical framework for improving the teaching performance in a school. The four stages are thus organisers for a set of associated improvement steps. But within these steps hides an established set of readings, activities, discussion points, together with key professional knowledge --- such as a common professional language[32] --- and techniques, which together form the basis of effective teaching. Feedback loops connected to student performance data provide benchmarks in the TPLI from which teaching improvement can be judged and intentions implemented. In latter stages of the TPLI roll-out the initiative has been assisted in this task by Hattie (2009) whose study indicates that a teaching effect size of 0.4 is the base-line for teaching performance or students are going backwards[33]. To this end, a set of guidelines has been developed to assist leaders when implementing the TPLI in their school. Further detail and an overview of the guidelines, which provide the detail on how to action each stage of the TPLI can be found in Doe, T. (2015) High Impact Instructional Leadership.

In summary then, the implementation of a Teacher Professional Learning Initiative must pay due attention to each of the three pillars and the three effect domains, as outlined in Figure 1. Collectively these illustrate the TPLI at work. Thus the deliberate

---

[32] In the case of the TPLI the common pedagogic language was Dimensions of Learning see: http://files.hbe.com.au/samplepages/197133.pdf

[33] See: http://www.slideshare.net/richardcookau/john-hattie-effect-sizes-on-achievement and http://www.teacherstoolbox.co.uk/T_effect_sizes.html

and intentional conceptualisation, design, and implementation of the TPLI encompass an ongoing and reflective consideration of the school and its state of readiness to enact each stage in the TPLI model.

What the Research says about the TPLI

Having briefly outlined the TPLI the task now is to conclude the chapter by reviewing research findings associated with it. To this end I reference my detailing to Doe, T. (2013) *A new way to think about teacher professional learning*. Primrose. Australia.

After 5 years implementing the TPLI in local schools in the Northern Territory, Australia, a qualitative study comprising interviews and surveys with teachers involved in the TPLI was conducted in 2003. Questions in the survey and the focus group interviews were organised according to a series of categories, which represented an element of the TPLI design and implementation strategy.

Data collected was then coded according to each category and through refining processes a series of themes emerged. These themes represent findings with respect to the TPLI and they are reported in the following sections.

With respect to the category of 'professional learning', which encompasses the learning intent of the TPLI, teachers tended to indicate that the TPLI had a positive impact on their teaching practice. One teacher (T23) commented, which was typical of most responses, "working together to improve and enhance learning outcomes for all of us was a great experience". Comments such as "everyone moving in the same direction creates a common sense of teacher collegiality" (T17), 'great stuff' (T2), and "great to see and hear conversations and teachers working in teams" (T14), were a common theme. However the majority of teachers (66%) did not yet see the full pedagogical value in the use of the 'common language of instruction', which was a key feature of the TPLI. There was evidence that indicated teachers were beginning to use the common language of instruction as a shared lens for Instructional Leadership, but responses tended to reflect a focus on their own classroom based problems.

When teachers were asked in the survey about their perceptions of the common language of instruction, the range of responses varied from 'confused' and 'informed' to 'excited'. Data indicated however that the TPLI had contributed to teachers' ability to work collegially, and had enhanced pedagogical conversations. With respect to the category of each teacher's 'individual professional learning needs' results tended to suggest that the TPLI developed a learning community which supported the teacher's own professional learning profile, however comments made by teachers tended to reinforce the need for the TPLI to give greater consideration to the priorities of their respective school. Teachers tended to make comments such as "professional learning needs to be complementary to the priorities of my school, rather than an additional, component of my workload" (T17).

This type of comment tended to reflect the pressures that incline traditional approaches to professional learning to focus on the system needs rather than that of the teacher's professional learning needs. 66% of surveyed teachers described the value of the TPLI in terms of its contribution to their school's overall approach to pedagogy and teacher planning. 60% also identified improvements in their teacher networks and in the relationship they had with the university as a result of their involvement in the TPLI. This tends to indicate that the TPLI is a useful mechanism in focusing a school to core teaching elements such as pedagogy and classroom planning, but also useful to universities in establishing meaningful teacher education relationships with schools and their teachers. However only 43% of teachers made comment that the TPLI created a useful way through which teachers could reflect on and improve their own practice: a core component of the TPLI.

Interestingly 90% made comment that the common language of instruction was most effective in enabling them to provide feedback and coaching to the teaching student and also enabled teachers to assist their teaching student to reflect on and improve their (the students) teaching practice. Further, when teachers were probed during interview about the common language of instruction outside the context of working with teaching students only 36% of teachers agreed (4% strong agreement) it was useful to them as teachers. Of those teachers (n=29 or 66%) who agreed that the common language of instruction provided a useful tool to improve their own teaching practice only 35% of these respondents (n=10), thought it had applicability for 'other schools' and their teachers.

On further analysis this tends to indicate that teacher perceptions about the common language of instruction are dependent upon a number of variables, ranging from their initial reasons for involvement in the TPLI (whether it was voluntary to be involved and not mandated) to the quality of the university TPLI facilitator (not all facilitators were highly valued by teachers and as such represents a deficiency that needs to be addressed in the TPLI program), to the alignment of the common language of instruction to each individual school's priorities. Examining the TPLI facilitator role further, data reveals that 90% of teachers either 'agree' or 'strongly agree' that it is the university TPLI facilitator who is a key variable in the quality of the TPLI. Further analysis of data indicated that there was a positive correlation between teachers who indicated the TPLIs positive impact on them and teachers who indicated their TPLI facilitator was of high quality.

Summary and Conclusions

The development of the TPLI was undertaken in response to contemporary schooling problems and issues as briefly outlined in an earlier section. The Teacher Professional Learning Initiative (TPLI) was designed to create opportunities to enhance teacher practice through professional learning. It would appear on balance that when the TPLI has 'first principle status' --- i.e. it is considered a priority by the school and as such is the through-line for the school's strategic intents and plans --- it can be a mechanism to improve the process of teacher professional learning in a school.

Since the TPLI facilitator --- the person who leads the TPLI in a school --- is a key component in the TPLI and in fostering the associated relationships with and between teachers, which are critical to the TPLI premise, the quality of the facilitator must be assured for overall TPLI effect. The study reveals the TPLI is efficacious in enabling practising teachers to work with student teachers. This is perhaps a reflection of the 'connecting' role that the common language of instruction plays with the teaching students university program and gives insight into the usefulness of a common language of instruction as a shared lens for 'learning to teach' purposes. In conclusion the greatest strength of the TPLI appears to be its capacity to create a networked learning community, which is considered crucial for practising teachers and student teachers alike.

The TPLI appears to be an effective mechanism for engaging teachers in the type of professional learning where collaboration acts to assist them in solving their teaching dilemmas, which lies at the heart of the reasons for which teachers will want to engage in a TPLI to improve their practice. The premise of enacting a common language of instruction through a TPLI arrangement is contingent on a number of variables, which when dealt with appropriately, may also prove effective in a TPLI type Instructional Leadership Model.

Taken together, the TPLI comes to represent a strategy that Schools and their teachers can co-opt when they plan their goal of becoming an outstanding school.

7. Using Learning Spaces and Arrangements to Enhance Teaching Performance

Jake Madden and David Lynch

> Chapters in this book outline the important role played by teachers in creating the outstanding school. But what is required of today's classrooms to enable teachers to effectively do their job and importantly for students to best learn? In this chapter we outline how, with key improvements in classroom design and the organization of teaching, that the traditional classroom environment can be reconfigured for teaching effect.

Introducing educational change can be problematic for school leaders as they must balance their energies on meeting institutional expectations, accountability requirements and the perceptions of the school's community that 'all is well'. This balance comes under strain however when school leaders are also charged with improving teaching. In simple terms this means enacting a 'change program' and from our own experiences this always comes with some kind of anxiety --- for all concerned --- which is further compounded by the many 'other' school-based challenges and obstructions that invariably surface.

Our point in Chapters 3, 5 and 6 was that any change agenda in schools requires the engagement of teachers to all facets of the change initiative but important for this book, that an increase in teaching capacity results and that performance is measured in student learning gains. In this chapter we explore the learning environment and associated teaching arrangements in the outstanding school. Our point is that like the requiring of new skills, teachers, and students for that matter, also need an appropriate environment in which to enact the business of teaching and learning.

Increasing the Teacher's Capacity to Deal with Individuals

Chapters to this point have firmly focused on the important role that teachers play in creating the outstanding school. Our defining of the outstanding school in Chapter 1, using the premise of 'every student achieving', is the inherent challenge in the quest to create this outstanding school. This in effect requires each teacher to have 'expert' teaching knowledge and skill but also the organizational scope and capacity to enact such an agenda.

As Chapters 2, 4, 5 and 8 detail, the single teacher in a single classroom is too limiting for such an agenda. One teacher working in isolation does not have the universal capacities to deal with the diversity of students that any given class (age related) cohort will comprise (Lynch, 2012; Hattie, 2009). To this end the *Collaborative Teacher Learning Model* (See Chapter 2) detailed how teachers need to operate in teams. This type of arrangement increases the teacher's teaching capacities on the one hand, while also embedding them in ongoing professional learning by virtue of their interactions with teaching peers on the other.

A study by Ronfeldt et al (2015) found that teachers who engage in collaboration tend to have better student achievement gains but importantly teachers also improve their teaching at greater rates. Working in teams is not without its challenges (Buckley, 2000) and thus further studies indicate that teachers need to be trained for such environments, but also leadership is required for optimal teaming effect (Sasson and Somech, 2014).

But taken on balance team teaching environments provide the

teacher with a strategic opportunity to increase their teaching capacities. But the traditional 9m x 9m 'privatised' classroom environment is an arrangement that makes teaming difficult.

Learning Spaces

Research indicates that a physical environment has a shaping influence not only on the interaction of students but also on the teaching of teachers (City, Elmore, Fiarman, & Teitel, 2009; Levine & Marcus, 2010). With this point in mind we now explore the premise of a required learning space for creating the outstanding school.

A learning space can be broadly defined as a place or the environment (classroom, workplace, on-line, meeting room, etc.) where learning takes place. Traditionally, the school classroom, with the teacher in their 'own' room, students in rows and facing a blackboard, with limited withdrawal spaces for individual or group learning activities, came to represent the industrial view of the 'compliant grade orientated school' and as such is how traditional learning environments were constituted.

This arrangement had the effect of teachers teaching in isolation to their peers and them being forced to engage in 'chalk and talks' or students' learning 'at single desks' for the majority of their teaching time. While we acknowledge 'direct instruction' can have high impact teaching results (Hattie, 2009) the constraints that this classroom arrangement represents invariably means the teaching scope and capacities of the teacher are also constrained (Madden, 2014, 2012). The goal in creating the foundations for the outstanding school we argue is increased capacities and flexible options. Further the options now available for learning with 'apps', on-line, e-learning, web surfing, web publishing and the like, also increase the opportunities for students. Let's explore these assertions a little further.

As Chapters 4 and 5 outlined, coaching, mentoring and feedback is a key element in engaging and then facilitating the improvement of each teacher's teaching. On another plane, as Chapter 8 will detail, the use of 'other teachers' and support staff in the teacher's classroom curriculum is a strategy for dealing with the multiples of students and their learning needs. A key point we made in an earlier section. Each however requires specific spaces and the standard classroom doesn't always universally suit. As with teachers and their teaching, studies also conclude that the makeup and use of the physical learning environment significantly affects student achievement (Blackmore et al., 2011).

Creating Required Learning Spaces and Places

As schools redesign their curriculums to meet the changing needs of its students and the teaching requirements of their teachers, the exploration and creation of appropriate learning spaces comes into focus when creating the outstanding school. This creation in effect comes to represent a cultural shift in teaching, as it is a move towards, what in effect are more flexible and 'open' spaces for teaching and learning. The consequence however is that teachers have to also learn new sets of teaching skills. A point we explore in greater detail in a section which follows (Jamieson, Fisher, Gilding, Taylor, & Trevitt, 2000).

Exploring the literature on what's required for these new learning spaces to be effective (see for example; Walker, et al., 2011; Brooks, 2011; Bissell, 2004; Blackmore, et al., 2011; Jamieson, et al., 2000; Lippincott, 2009) the following attributes, for teachers and students alike, emerges:

- A convergence of the physical and virtual learning environments into a cohesive 'place and space' for learning and teaching.

- Arrangements that enable a combination of collaboration and individual endeavour depending upon the curriculum agenda.
- The extension of opportunity to learn beyond the classroom, but in a connected and informed way.
- Spaces to innovate, ideate, create, and consolidate learnings either as an individual or a group.
- Arrangements that enable each student to learn at a pace and in a context that meets their specific individual learning goals.
- Mechanisms and facilities which enable various data sources to be accessed, processed and interrogated for teaching effect.

But the important message to come from the associated literature is that while such spaces and their incumbent facilities create opportunities for increased teaching capacities and perhaps more engaged learning and teaching activities, these spaces are no substitute for good teaching (OECD, 2009; Walker, et al, 2011; Hattie, 2009).

Changing Pedagogies

At the heart of such 'new' and 'flexible' learning spaces is the generation of teaching and learning activities which are tailored to mirror the profile of work and life in the Knowledge Economy. Consequently, project based learning, assigned or student generated research projects, virtual activities, discovery activities, experimentations and the like begin to emerge in the classroom curriculum. These new activities also enable and complement teacher collaborations where teachers join forces to design and thus deal with the diversity of learning goals that are represented in cohorts of students in a school. These collaborations we refer to as 'cohort learning' and the premise was illustrated in the *Collaborative Teacher Learning Model* outlined in Chapter 2.

Implementing a cohort approach effectively means responsibility for student learning rests equally with each teacher in a particular grade [or cohort]. The shared decision-making on student learning in such arrangements therefore shifts into a series of associated collaborative teaching teams, where student groupings are based upon individual learning needs. This collaborative structure allows instruction to be matched to each student. The learning environment thus creates the required space for such teaching and learning work to occur (Madden et al., 2012, p. 21).

Moving from a traditional 'one teacher – one class – one classroom' grade level (for primary) or subject based (for high school) structure to a cohort-learning-centred approach situated in flexible learning spaces not only enabled staff in our 'pilot school' in Chapter 2 to deal with student diversity but also became **the** catalyst for the activation of the associated coaching, mentoring and feedback regime. According to Lackney and Jacobs (2002) there is a direct relationship between learning spaces and the collaboration of teachers. The pilot school detailed in Chapter 2 also reflected this finding. Research into learning spaces further indicates that teachers who regularly collaborate tend to be more reflective and thus more inclined to modify their classroom curriculums as a regular part of their teaching practice as student learning needs change (OECD, 2009; Bissell, 2004).

A further outcome generated by creating such flexible spaces and the emergence of an aligned collaborative teaching culture, is an increase in teacher capacity for differentiation. In simple terms these arrangements appear to encourage teachers to take collective responsibility for **all students** in the cohort--- as a team of teachers—and thus design and be assured of the required capacity to deal with the confluence student need. But moving teachers towards such a position requires leadership and guidance. To this end we are assisted by Tomlinson (2003; 2000; 1999) who suggests teaching is enhanced in a cohort learning situation by:

- <u>Clarification of Key Concepts:</u> Teachers are able to introduce the intent of each lesson and when breaking into small groups provides for deep understanding of the content at the students' required level.

- <u>Promoting Student Choice:</u> Balancing the need for curricula driven learning, operating in a cohort arrangement can allow students choice in both content and teacher instruction.

- <u>Process-Based Student Supports:</u> Enhancing opportunities for student learning, teachers are able to provide scaffolding, pairing of students with more proficient peers, cross-aged tutors and differentiated materials in order to meets student learning needs.

- <u>Engaging All Students Through Varied Learning Tasks:</u> In cohort teaching and learning the ease of varying learning tasks to engage the diversity of learners is spread amongst the class teachers. Whether students are auditory, visual, tactile or kinaesthetic learners, teachers can scaffold learning to meet student needs.

- <u>Use of Assessment as a Teaching Tool:</u> Working together in a shared space offers opportunity for assessment to be used as an ongoing teaching tool rather than merely measuring) student achievement. (Tomlinson & Allan, 2000; Tomlinson et al., 2003; Tomlinson, 1999)

As we indicated in an earlier section, such flexible and predominately 'open' spaces support the establishment of the coaching, mentoring and feedback (CMF) regime outlined in Chapters 4 and 5, by enabling teachers to observe their colleagues in action. In simple terms there are 'no walls', in either the physical or classroom teaching sense in such arrangements and as such teachers begin to coalesce their engagements around conversations about 'what's needed in teaching'. In effect this circumstance paves the way for a set of ongoing professional dialogues on one's teaching practice, especially as it generally moves towards immediate feedback.

To this point in the chapter we have focused on teachers and the outcomes for them in terms of their teaching capacities. While the thesis of this book has focused concerns to ensuring learning outcome achievement in all students as the benchmark for teaching performance, we now briefly detail the specific benefits for students in such flexible and open learning environments for points of reference. From the associated literature (see for example; Walker, et al., 2011; Brooks, 2011; Blackmore, et al., 2011; Lippincott, 2009; Bissell, 2004; Jamieson, et al, 2000) we make the following findings:

- Students develop collaborative/co-operative skills when these are modelled by their class teacher in such arrangement and which appear to enable students to become better collaborative learners;
- Students become more responsible for their own learning and thus more able to communicate elements, which further enable the teacher to respond to them.
- The scope that such open and flexible arrangements present to teachers enables them to develop more inventive and tailored learning activities, with the consequence that students are more engaged and less likely to be disruptive.

So what are the principles required to create these new learning environments?

In previous sections we've described the notion of the requirement for new learning spaces: those that are flexible and open. The premise of single teacher rooms being remodelled to create large and enabled spaces, with nooks for individual work and tools to enable teachers to teach and students to learn probably becomes the visual. And for us this visual is sound. But in coming to the design of such spaces requires a series of principles which focus the school to achieving the desired teaching and learning effect.

In achieving design intents when creating open and flexible learning environments, we are assisted by Brown (2015) who has created seven design principles for classrooms. Taken together his principles come to represent what needs to be considered when designing the required teaching/learning environment:

- Principle 1: Design aligns with the campus context
- Principle 2: Planning and design process involved those who will use it and informed by an evidence base
- Principle 3: Support and operations: how will the environment be maintained and that the imagined course gets full benefit from such designs?
- Principle 4: Environmental quality: the health and welfare of users
- Principle 5: Layout and furnishings that meet planned activities within.
- Principle 6: Tools and technology that mesh with planned activities within
- Principle 7: Innovation - avoid not just tinkering with what is already in place (Brown, 2015, p.1)

Summary

In this chapter we provided an introduction to the concept of required learning environments for creating the outstanding school. We have also offered a practical insight into how such 'open and flexible' teaching environments enable the establishment of a coaching, mentoring and feedback regime to focus and engage teachers to teaching improvement. A key aspect of such prescribed learning environments is a cultural shift that occurs whereby teachers are able to collectively respond to the broad range of student needs.

Flexible learning spaces coupled with the pedagogical "cohort" approach (Madden, 2012) to teaching and learning has, from research as outlined in Chapter 2, enabled the school to more effectively address and focus upon student learning outcomes (Madden et al., 2012). Design principles as reported by Brown (2015) provide a scaffold for the school when designing the required learning environment.

In conclusion the collaborative classroom fosters a greater sense of school professional community, allowing students to experience and imitate the cooperative, collaborative skills that teachers model as they co-teach. These skills are often cited as essential ones for students' future success in school and in knowledge age careers. However, as this chapter has indicated, this type of new teaching and learning activity requires an appropriate environment. Taken together, this chapter has detailed another piece of the creating the outstanding school 'pie'.

8. Developing the Outstanding Lesson

David Lynch and Richard Smith

This chapter explores the premise of *designing the outstanding lesson*. To this end the chapter provides an insight into the Learning Management Process (LMP)[34]. In simple terms the LMP is a set of teaching design questions that orientate the teacher to the development of effective lessons. The LMP has had a successful history in the preparation of quality teachers at both the undergraduate and post graduate education levels, with its intuitive 'design questions' providing valuable pedagogic prompts and associated reference guides. In effect the LMP takes the teacher back to basics when designing the outstanding lesson.

In this chapter we explore the premise of *designing the outstanding lesson*. To achieve this goal we begin with a series of introductory statements to locate the premise of what we argue is required in 'teaching planning'. This is followed by a brief insight into the 'teaching design idea' before we provide an expose into the Learning Management Process (LMP). This expose reveals a set of 'design' steps and suggests further readings for developing the effective lesson or global classroom curriculum. The LMP has had a successful history in the preparation of quality teachers at both the undergraduate and post graduate education spheres, with its intuitive 'design questions' proving valuable prompts as the teacher 'designs' their teaching activities (Lynch, 2012; Smith and Lynch, 2010; Ingvarson, et al, 2005). We turn now to some brief introductory statements.

---

[34] The Learning Management Process was developed by David Lynch in 1998.

The Premise of a Rethought Planning Process

We begin by stating that our view is that a school will only ever be as good as the sum of its teachers' teaching capacities. Put another way, if the goal is to create the outstanding school, then it's the quality of each teacher's teaching that has to come into sharp focus (see Mourshed, et al., 2010; Smith and Lynch, 2010; Hattie, 2009). Take this notion a step further and this focus must sharpen to the lessons that are planned and the pedagogic strategies deployed therein by each teacher.

In making these opening comments, we effectively point to what we see as the common weakness in schools, the lack of pedagogical approach detail. More specifically, we note through many years of research in the area, that the teacher, in a teaching planning phase, tends not to state the pedagogical strategies they plan to use beyond general statements about learning activities and similar glosses (see for example, Madden and Lynch, 2014; Lynch, 2012; Lynch and Smith, 2011; Smith and Lynch, 2010). There's a certain taken for 'grantedness' that appears to circumvent any need for such pedagogic design detail, which in turn, tends to encourage the teacher to teach on the whim of their intuitions. In our view this loose approach fundamentally dilutes the teacher's capacity for achieving learning outcomes in **all** students (Lynch, 2012; Smith and Lynch, 2010, 2006;). Further, just creatively making up classroom activity to engage students in is no guarantee of learning outcome success either. Nor is assigning students set tasks and then supervising them from afar. This in our minds is tantamount to a surgeon wheeling a patient into an operating theatre and then handing the patient the scalpel. Teachers, like a surgeon may assign their charges 'follow-up' activities to enhance their outcomes, but the planks of what needs to be done is always explicitly planned and then expertly executed by the professional. Nothing is left to chance and it is always focused on the peculiarities of **the individuals concerned**. Our view is that effective teaching is a highly technical process and the knowledge underpinning should not be discernable to the untrained eye. Many people may teach in our society, but it is the trained teaching professional who has the capacities to design teaching segments and achieve the inherent outcomes in *all* students every time. To these ends we shape this chapter.

It is not difficult to appreciate then that no matter how excellent the curriculum content, its success depends on the implementation of **teaching strategies** that achieve the desired outcomes. So what the teacher does --- their respective teaching strategy competence --- becomes the core issue in curriculum development and planning, and its 'referencing' to a teaching evidence base is a critical ingredient. This evidence base represents highly specialized teaching knowledge and well-honed teaching expertise for success: success referenced to an evidence base. Hattie (2009) is at pains to make this point.

Pulling all this together, our central point is that research evidence indicates that **what the teacher does while teaching** is the most powerful influence in learning. According to current evidence, and despite current teaching practices, teaching strategies in **a direct or explicit instruction approach** are the most effective tools a teacher can possess (see Hattie, 2009, p.238; Hattie, 2005, 2003). Pedagogical strategies then should be made explicit in curriculum development and planning models. The structural, content, resource and procedural matters in curriculum planning models are important, but our contention is that *teaching strategies* are the *primary concern* of the professional teacher. Our view is that most traditional curriculum development and planning models need a rethink to bring them into line with what is presently known about the effects of teachers and teaching on student achievement. This conclusion is important in the context of creating the outstanding school.

Having now made these introductory comments, we now turn to the specifics of this chapter.

The Teaching Design Idea

There are many curriculum design frameworks available for teachers to choose from. While they are all focused on achieving a teaching starting point --- that being the development of a classroom curriculum plan for the teacher to reference their work to --- most provide little guidance as to the success elements and the specificity that each requires for teaching success. We thus prefer the idea of *designing* teaching over "planning". It implies that the teacher:

(i) is **actively engaged** in achieving definite, articulated outcomes,

(ii) intends that he or she and the students **do particular things** in order to accomplish the outcomes,

(iii) identifies and selects **optimal strategic pathways** to reach the outcomes, especially empirical justified pedagogical strategies,

(iv) consciously checks out what his/her student's background knowledge, attitudes and behaviours that are **pre-requisites to success,**

(v) establishes **performance standards** and the means for collecting data to demonstrate student standards, and

(vi) uses such performance data to determine their success as a teacher.

Under this kind of regime, teachers can begin to be confident in their capacity to do their work, while knowing that nothing is guaranteed. In previously published ideas about teaching design, Smith and Lynch (2006) contended:

> Like any other professional with the obligation to deliver health, legal, architectural, dental or optical services for clients, teachers are obligated to deliver learning services at an appropriate standard to their students and their families. **Teachers are not free to do what they choose, because**

there is an expectation that the services will be successful (Smith and Lynch, 2006, p. 54, emphasis added).

We expand this contention by adding that the purchasers of education, its principal investors, parents and students, still expect today, that education should result in greater knowledge. In a Knowledge Society, where qualifications and capacity to apply what is known are highly valued, success at school now has enormous implications for the future well-being of most individuals and society. It is apparent then that intentional pedagogical design that achieves learning outcomes for all students must lie at the heart of a professional teacher's repertoire of knowledge and skill.

The teaching design idea is the core idea that guides our comments about teaching in the remainder of the chapter. It diametrically opposes the idea of the proliferation of "personal" teaching pedagogies based on individual preference, characteristic of traditional teaching practices and is very much focused on the teacher engaged in teaching; not just supervising supposed acts that may result in learning (Smith and Lynch, 2010). This is not meant as a slight on teachers, but a comment about the profession at all levels. Consider these examples:

Miss White spends endless hours preparing interesting activities for her Year One class to do. Her classroom is a joy to behold with children's art and language work displayed on the walls, on-going science and SOSE projects occupying corners and ceiling space. Children's days are spent preparing and creating displays and working in groups. It is, to all intents and purposes, a children's paradise. Parents are impressed with displays, colour and the obvious commitment to the children's environment.

And

Mr Brown, sits at his desk at the front of his class while his charges are busily engaged in some kind of activity. At his command students slip seamlessly from one subject to the other and there is little noise emanating from his room and students are seldom referred to the school's administration. He is by all accounts firmly in control. Mr Brown has always been assigned to the 'problem' classes because his capacity to create order where there was none is seen as a mark of an experienced teacher: especially by a busy school administration.

We are of course supportive of such classrooms at one level, BUT we ask do they achieve defined outcomes in every student? However, we are bound to challenge the effectiveness of "activity" and "control" oriented teaching because:

> As educators, we would need to be sure that the students were enjoying worthwhile learning, that various activities and topics were rank ordered according to their importance, and that students were achieving intended outcomes. We would want to be sure that students had some advance organisers and knew what was expected of them while they participated in the activities. Moreover we would want to know that the children were engaged in the same curriculum as most others in the system and how well they achieved the curriculum outcomes; not just that they had. We would also want to know about the kinds of understanding they were developing and the kinds of personal capacities they were creating as a result of being in the classroom. In short, interesting and controlled classroom 'activities' are necessary, **but they are not sufficient if the expectation is that most children will reach the requirements of the mandated syllabuses and be prepared for an emergent society**. The job of 'teaching' at all levels is more complex and demanding than making up diverse activities, irrespective of how long those activities may take the teacher to prepare and administer (Smith and Lynch, 2006, p. 54, emphasis added).

Our key point is that teaching is an active process where the applied strategies are explicit to the defined learning intents and firmly focused on the profile of students. By this we mean the teacher is responsible for ensuring that each student achieves the designated learning outcomes and their performance is judged on learning achievement data. The emphasis here is on the student rather than on the teacher and his or her attributes. The teacher's orientation is primarily focussed on points (i)-(vi) noted earlier: content, teaching strategies, achievable performance standards and the personal and social capacities that students develop for later life. While the specifications for achieving learning outcomes in all students cannot be applied in a mechanistic manner, the existing research evidence indicates what teaching strategies have a high probability of achieving successful learning outcomes (Hattie, 2012; 2009; Smith and Lynch, 2010, 2006).

So, in both its procedural and creative phases, the premise of designing teaching is then a process in which the various elements are arranged and orchestrated. While teachers may be familiar with a process of 'situational analysis', the 'Learning Management Process' that we outline in a later section builds on that process, by entailing a quite specific technical knowledge, sequential steps and process guidance and a clear set of goals on the part of the teacher. Putting a design together for a particular set of students and in settings that are framed with constraints such as time and resources requires high levels of organisational knowledge and skill. It involves detailed knowledge and analysis of what has gone before, what comes next and how this particular segment links the two and why. This is why we refer to teaching as "Learning Management:" i.e. "designs with intent".

For more information on the Learning Management concept we recommend:

Smith, R. & Lynch, D. (2010). *Rethinking teacher education: Teacher education in the knowledge age.* Sydney, NSW: AACLM Press.

The Learning Management Process

The LMP represents a rethink of the various curriculum development models that are available to teachers, especially in under-graduate teaching courses. Teachers fundamentally use the *Learning Management Process* (LMP) for two inter-related reasons. First, to embed themselves in an evidence based and inquiry mindset and second, to develop their classroom curriculum. The LMP is captured by 8 key questions, which are organised by three developmental phases: *Outcomes, Strategy and Evidence* (see Figure 1). Each phase has a select series of **teaching design questions**. The teacher develops a classroom curriculum (i.e. a single lesson, sequence of lessons or a unit of work) by engaging with each phase and its questions and recording 'findings' (or answers) in some kind of easily referable plan form. Each phase thus contains focal questions that provide the teacher with the material to develop a classroom curriculum.

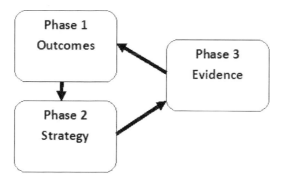

Figure 1: The Component Pieces of the Learning Management Design Process.

The LMP is analogous to building a house. There is vision or a desire for what is to be achieved; for what the house will look like; how the internal and external arrangements will be configured to meet the vision or construction brief and so on. This series is a parallel to setting *outcomes*.

Once the outcomes have been specified, the builder enacts a set of strategies that reflect the standards of their profession and the circumstance of the building site in order to achieve those outcomes. This phase can be termed *strategy*. Once built, the home-owner ascertains whether or not the house has been built to the required specified standards. This process we can term the collection of *evidence*. The amalgam of these three phases becomes *the plan*, the classroom curriculum in teaching parlance. The plan is then followed logically, despite inevitable difficulties from the environment and probably resource constraints, to achieve the outcomes as set. Should the finished house not meet the outcomes, either during construction or after construction, then a process of *diagnostics* is employed to ascertain why there are apparent defects or the house has failed to meet the set outcomes. The scope of this chapter does not extend to diagnostics, but readers can expand their knowledge of the LMP by reading Lynch and Smith (2011).

Applying the Learning Management Process

In this section, the eight questions, which comprise the LMP, are explained as a step-by-step guide to developing the classroom curriculum. More detailed information is available from:

Lynch, D. and Smith, R. (2011) *Designing the Classroom Curriculum in the Knowledge Age,* AACLM Press: Sydney

The first point to note when enacting the LMP is that the process is question-based. This means the 'answers', when recorded effectively in plan form, become the classroom curriculum. Of course, not all answer information fits a template (see the appendix for a sample lesson template build for the LMP) and is better used as reference and background information. Making appendices for later reference is recommended in this case. While it is imperative that such appendices are made it's the inherent inquiry process that each requires for compilation that is paramount in the overall process.

While the learning management questions are presented in numerical order, Question 1, 2, 3 and so on, it is the *phases* that dictate the order in which the questions are answered. Question numbers are for reference purposes (see Figure 1 for the phases). Therefore, on entering a phase, consider each set of questions as an inter-related group. Answers to any one question are thus affected by the other associated questions.

It is important first to discuss how the answers to the learning management questions are formatted. The LMP is a generic learning management design 'template' that can be constituted as a lesson plan, a series of lessons or unit of work. We substitute the term 'classroom curriculum' for learning management plan in this chapter. Depending on the classroom curriculum development context, the format of the learning management plan will vary but the questions stay the same. The scope of the chapter does allow for such elaborations but Lynch and Smith (2012) is a recommended further reading.

From the outset, and especially from the perspective of the novice teacher, the application of the Learning Management Process (LMP) appears daunting. There are many considerations and the time to extract and format such information is considerable. This reflects the sophistication of the knowledge required to be successful in teaching. But if a teacher wants *all students* to make the required learning gains, then a thorough application of the process seems imperative. But there is light at the end of the tunnel as the following explains.

Being a capable and experienced teacher means that the process is eventually internalised, not unlike how a dentist knows instinctively the rudiments of various dental procedures and the likely scenarios for procedures and recovery. Accumulated experience in this learning management approach enables a teacher to reduce planning time to fit curriculum programming needs. That is to say, the capable experienced teacher who knows the process uses it as part of their everyday professional repertoire.

The 8 Learning Management Questions

In the three sections that follow, each Learning Management Question is explained in its numerical order. Each design phase is presented to provide an overview of key information relating to the phase and its associated questions. Figure 1 provides an overview of each 'question' and their central focus. The commentary for each question is brief to enable an easy flow of design information. Should you require more information you should refer to Lynch and Smith (2011), as it elaborates each question and its associated steps. We now discuss the 8 Learning Management Design Questions, commencing with Phase 1 Outcomes and Learning Management Question 1.

Phase	Question	Focus
Outcomes	LMQ1: What have my students achieved to date ?	Ascertaining Student Readiness for Teaching
	LMQ2: What do I aim to achieve in my students?	Defining the Learning outcomes
Strategy	LMQ3. How do my students' best Learn?	Evidence Based Best Practice and the learning peculiarities of the cohort
	LMQ4: What resources do I have at my disposal?	The Means
	LMQ5: What are my Teaching Strategies?	The Application of Evidence Based Strategies to achieve the defined learning outcomes (LMQ2)
	LMQ6. Who will do what to support the teaching strategy?	Human / Support Resources / Teaching Teams
Evidence	LMQ7. How will I check that students have achieved the defined learning outcomes?	Assessment
	LMQ8. How will I report student progress?	Reporting

Figure 1: The 8 Learning Management Questions

Let's now explore the 8 learning management questions in more detail.

The Learning management Questions Explained

LMQ1: What have my students achieved to date?
Ascertaining Student Readiness

LMQ1 identifies the student's current state of achievement and the goal in answering this question is to benchmark each student's teaching readiness. This question is answered with reference to the expectations of a syllabus (its indicators, benchmarks, work samples) and the outcome of the question is a starting point for your teaching. To this end each student is classified as 'at standard' or 'requiring special consideration'.

When developing a curriculum plan for any class cohort a first consideration is always the *teaching readiness* of students. As you will appreciate in the next question when assigning learning outcomes in Learning Management Question 2 (LMQ2), the Syllabus is a chief reference for what you aim to achieve in each student. Considering these points together then, the task in Learning Management Question 1 (LMQ1) is to ascertain *what a student already knows* as a first analysis of their *readiness for teaching* and to establish a starting and end point for teaching (i.e. in LMQ2 where the learning outcomes are set).

The 'At Standard' and 'Requiring Special Consideration' benchmarking terminology is an organising mechanism for teaching in a year or grade level classroom context.

> *"At standard students"* *we defined as those who are in an age-related cohort and achieve at the prescribed level. These students are thus ready for the teaching program as outlined in LMQ2.*

> *"Special consideration students"* *we defined as those students who are in an age-related cohort, but* **not** *achieving at the prescribed level due to an identified reason. These students require special consideration for a variety of reasons including: gifted and talented, learning disability or difficulty, disengagement from a particular content or subject area etc. These students are not ready for the teaching program as planned and will need to be supported by customised program modification or separate individual programs. LMQ6 provides strategy for dealing with students in this category by way of 'collaborative teaching teams'.*

Teachers start the LMP by considering the 'at standard' students first. Modifications to the developed classroom curriculum are made according to the profile of each requiring special consideration (RSC) student and the organisation to accommodate RSC student is facilitated in subsequent questions. In cases where the RSC student requires major modifications the teacher should develop a stand along individual education program (IEP) using the LMP as the guide. Most schools have templates that will assist in this process.

The Steps to Follow

Step 1. Review the appropriate (subject) syllabus document to acquaint yourself with the rationale, content, performance indicators/ benchmarks and developmental steps that inform the achieving of the prescribed learning outcomes therein.

Step 2: Generate, (gather) student learning performance evidence so as to create a comprehensive learning profile for each student.

Conduct pre-tests and review work samples and the like to strengthen this profile. At a more sophisticated level teachers create a base-line of student data from which they can determine their teaching effect size [35]

Step 3: Review the profile of each student and, in reference to the syllabus and its various support addendums, benchmark each student on their teaching readiness. The cumulative result of this benchmarking is the starting point for designing your teaching/ instruction (at LMQ5) and a base line for assessing learning progress (at LMQ7).

You should now have a list of 'at standard students' who are ready for the planned instruction, together with another list of students who will require modifications to fit the overall learning intent – 'requiring special considerations'.

Step 4: Record the information you have compiled as a series of *key* dot points summaries and locate the support information in a Student Performance Portfolio for ongoing teaching reference. Each student should now be identified as 'at standard' or 'requiring special consideration' .

NOTE: LMQ1, when complete, is thus a summary of key findings on all students and will inform your teaching goals in LMQ2: where learning outcomes are set.

NOTE: Classroom teachers usually develop and maintain a *Student Performance Portfolio*. This portfolio is a set of files on each student and contains work samples that are performance benchmarked. Information collected as part of LMQ1 should be summarised and stored in such a portfolio.

---

[35] For more information on teaching effect sizes review: http://www.teacherstoolbox.co.uk/T_effect_sizes.html or read Hattie (2009)

LMQ2: What do I aim to achieve in my students?

Defining the Learning outcomes

LMQ2 is about setting the learning outcomes for the classroom curriculum. These learning outcomes are the chief focus for the classroom curriculum and are used as a reference in all subsequent learning management question responses. Particular reference is made to these *LMQ2 statements* at LMQ 5 (the specific teaching strategies) and LMQ7 (the assessment strategy).

Learning outcomes in the classroom situation have a predominately formal basis and so a *Subject Syllabus* is the point of reference when establishing formal learning outcomes in classrooms. Your findings in LMQ1 indicate where you should start teaching, while LMQ2 indicates what you should aim to achieve in students --- the learning outcomes --- in a given time period, by way of classroom curriculum (for example, by the end of a school term or year). LMQ2 defines the goals or success indicators and signals the content of the curriculum plan. It therefore becomes the starting point, in a backward mapping activity, for the learning strategies that are detailed in LMQ5. It is important that the learning outcomes statements are right because they have an impact on the LMQs that follow.

It is important to understand that the learning outcomes outlined in various syllabus documents are complex in that each one comes to represent a series of hierarchical and thus inter-related knowledge bits that require specific teaching steps to be achieved in students. Given the broad scope of knowledge (the content) to be achieved in each syllabus learning outcome, the teacher needs to 'break' each syllabus learning outcome into instructional 'bits' before commencing specific *daily teaching segments*. Syllabus *Indicators* can be used to frame these instructional 'bits' --- which in effect represent the inherent knowledge hierarchy. The result of this task is that LMQ2 is written as a focal syllabus learning outcome(s) and then a listing of sequential instructional (i.e. more specific) learning outcomes (ILOs). These ILOs then create a direct connection to outlined teaching strategies and assessments (LMQ7).

The Steps to Follow

Step 1: Familiarize yourself with the 'subject' syllabus and its defined learning outcomes

NOTE: Ensure you have personal knowledge competency with the knowledge you are to teach. This competency extends to understanding the hierarchy of knowledge that sequentially represents the overall defined syllabus learning outcome.

Step 2: In reference to LMQ1 decide the 'learning outcomes' that fit your student profile and the intent of the subject syllabus.

NOTE: Don't be tempted to just start teaching without referencing your student's readiness.

Step 3: Analyse each chosen learning outcome(s) to identify the knowledge content to be taught and the teaching sequence each represents. This analysis should result in the listing of a series of numbered (use a referencing code) 'instructional learning outcomes' (or sub-syllabus learning outcomes) prefaced by the sentence stem: *"The students will be able to:"* which provides specific focus to what you have to plan to teach. Taken together, the sum of instructional

learning outcomes come to represent the parent syllabus learning outcome.

NOTE: An instructional learning outcome is best written with one key verb that creates specificity e.g. Estimate volume in 'cups', and 'objects of standard measure'

Step 4: Record the proceeds of each step using an appropriate Template.

Example:

LMQ2: What do I aim to achieve in my students?
My student will be able to:

SLO: Estimates, measures, compares and records volumes and capacities using litres, millilitres and cubic centimetres
(Procedural Knowledge):
P1: Estimate volume in 'cups', and 'objects of standard measure'
P2: Use a measuring container to 'measure' volumes of objects
(Declarative Knowledge)
D1: Explain the need for formal units when measuring volume
D2: Recognise that a litre can occur in various shapes
D3: Distinguish between mass and volume
D4: Recognise everyday items measured in volumes
D5: Understand that solids are measured in cm3 and volumes in litres/ millilitres

---

LMQ3. How do my students best Learn?
Evidence Based Best Practice

LMQ3 is about engaging with the 'best practice' in a given subject (i.e. mathematics) and meshing this with the learning peculiarities of the student cohort (i.e. bilingual, limited schooling, cultural aspects, etc.).

By answering LMQ3 you identify appropriate evidence-based information to support an understanding of how students' best learn and you can best teach the specific subject. Without LMQ3, teachers are caught in a cycle of attempting to do the same better whereas the learning management design message is that effective practice is doing better by knowing what is best. The question specifically engages the teacher to:

- **Review evidence-based best practice** research as it relates to the subject that is to be taught.
- **Factor the specific learning needs and peculiarities** of the target student/learning cohort as context for dealing with students.
- Consider the required **Habits of Mind and Attitudes and Perceptions** for the knowledge to be taught (see Marzano and Pickering, 2006)

The Steps to Follow

Step 1: Review evidence based best practice considerations that apply to the Subject (subject area) you are teaching in.

Step 2: Reflect on the information you gleaned as part of LMQ1 to ascertain what specific strategies are required to support the peculiarities of students.

> NOTE: Factor these findings as you engage with LMQ5: teaching strategies

Step 3: Record findings as dot point summaries and link these through a coding system to a portfolio of evidence/materials or as links to reference materials for ongoing referral.

LMQ4: What resources do I have at my disposal?

The Means

LMQ4 is the point at which the teacher identifies what is available to support the classroom curriculum. LMQ4 sets the parameters for classroom teaching resources, giving consideration to the fact that teachers operate within a framework of limited resources. These constraints encourage entrepreneurial activity. It is through Question 4 that the wide range of resources: physical (including time allocations), financial and technological are audited in preparation for teaching. Human resources are considered here but are planned in greater details as part of LMQ6.

The Steps to Follow

Step 1: Identify the resources that best practice and the subject requires.

Step 2: Record findings as a list of things to have 'readied' for teaching support.

LMQ5: What are my Teaching Strategies?

The Application of Evidence Based Strategies to achieve the defined Learning Outcomes (LMQ2)

LMQ5 is the point at which the teacher decides and then records the teaching strategies that are a best fit to the defined learning outcomes (LMQ2) in a context of the overall circumstance of the classroom curriculum (LMQ1, LMQ3, LMQ4, LMQ6). This task is complete when there is an outlining of sequential and explicit teaching steps. We hasten to add that this 'step' is fundamentally important in the outstanding lesson agenda. This step requires the implementation of 'research based teaching practices' for overall learning gain effect. To this end we suggest you refer to the *'Dimensions of Learning Manual'* *(Marzano and Pickering, 2006)* as this provides explicit teaching step design guidance. For an on-line copy: *http://www.ascd.org/ASCD/pdf/siteASCD/publications/books/Dimensions-of-Learning-Teachers-Manual-2nd-edition.pdf*

LMQ5 is the actual *teaching design stage* where the classroom curriculum, from the 'teaching' perspective, is conceptualized and later used as the teaching reference to follow. LMQ5 is completed on two levels. The first level is the overall plan for teaching during a school year / term, the Year or *Term Plan*. In this phase the scope of the curriculum is explored and timetabled for teaching across the year/ term.

The second level is the specific detailing of teaching strategies for a lesson (or series of lessons). This level is really the 'nitty gritty' of teacher's work. There are five key 'back-grounding' considerations involved in answering this question on both levels.

1. Use the answers to the previous LM questions (i.e. 1 through 4) to frame the development of your lesson.
2. Assign Instructional Learning Outcomes (from LMQ2) to **each** teaching episode, as this focuses you to what has to be achieved in students.
3. Know the knowledge hierarchy that each instructional learning outcome (LMQ2) represents, so you can sequentially teach to it.
4. Know the stage of development that each instructional learning outcome represents in students (see Table 2).
5. Incorporate lesson design elements and prompts as outlined in Figure 3. This outlining provides a framework for developing the specific lesson steps/ strategies.

The Extent of Knowledge Held by students	The Teaching Focus Required
The knowledge to be learned (LMQ2) is **new** to students	Enable students to <u>acquire and integrate</u> new knowledge they are learning.
Basic conceptual knowledge (LMQ2) **has been learned** by students but requires further development	Enable students to <u>extend and refine</u> knowledge they are learning.
The knowledge (LMQ2) has been developed in students, but **needs extending** through meaningful application	Enable students to <u>apply what they are learning meaningfully</u>.
For more information see: http://www.ascd.org/ASCD/pdf/siteASCD/publications/books/Dimensions-of-Learning-Teachers-Manual-2nd-edition.pdf	

Table 2: Knowledge and Stage of Development in students

Key Element	Sample Teaching Strategy Attributes
The initial lesson design focus	Will there be evidence of "We Are Learning To…" (WALT)? Will it relate to what the students were doing? Will the students be able to answer questions at the end of the lesson? Is it connected to prior learning?
An Initiating Strategy/starter/hook:	The goal of the lesson is outlined to students to focus them Students are engaged with the lesson goal. Students are actively thinking about the lesson – connecting previous knowledge.
Limit Teacher Talk/student centered:	Instruction is concise and explicit. The students are quickly engaged in action/thinking activities. Appropriate vocabulary is used and scaffolded for understanding.
Use of Graphic Organisers	Students record/summarise/categorise information during the lesson. Information is gathered and presented using a graphic organizer.

	The graphic organiser engages higher order thinking.
Differentiated Groups:	Instruction is set at students' level (LMQ1)
	While there is a place for individual work on 'tasks' the majority of time should be in small groups – the focus is intimate.
	Feedback is structured and immediate.
	LMQ6 is factored for effect
Active Movement:	Students are working collaboratively and spaces for learning are flexible.
	The structure and strategies allow interaction
Higher Order Questions/critical thinking (ATLs):	Students are challenged through the use of higher order questions such as Blooms
Summarise/plenary:	Each lesson has reflective time for students to record/summarise (reflect) on their learning.
	When writing their thoughts/reflections, is it connected to the WALT?
For further information: Marzano, R., Pickering, D., & Pollock, J. E. (2001). *Classroom instruction that works: Research-based strategies for increasing student achievement.* Alexandra, VA: Association for Supervision and Curriculum Development	

Figure 3: Sample Elements in the Effective Lesson[36]

The Steps to Follow

Step 1: Refer to the instructional learning outcomes (ILO) assigned at LMQ2.

Step 2: Consider the following for teaching strategy effect:
- **Figures 2 and 3**

---

[36] Sourced from Jake Madden, 2015 from Dar Al Marefa Private School's 'Effective Lesson Foci'

- 'Dimensions of Learning Manual' (Marzano and Pickering, 2006)
- 'Classroom Instruction that Works: Research-based strategies for increasing student achievement (Marzano, R., Pickering, D., & Pollock, J. E. 2001) and begin to conceptualise sequential teaching steps which collectively work towards the achievement of EACH learning outcome (LMQ2).

Step 3: Using the supplied template (appendix) list the instructional steps you will follow to achieve the ILO.

NOTE: These 'Instructional Learning Outcomes' provide the sequential reference for achieving each SLO and as such the role of the teacher at this stage is to elaborate their teaching actions by outlining specific steps that align with each instructional learning outcome in order.

Example:

Instructional Learning Outcome (from LMQ2)	What I will do (the teaching Steps)
D1	Step 1: Explain—Provide a student-friendly description, explanation, and example of the new terms to be learnt.
D2	Step 2: Restate—Ask students to restate the description, explanation or example in their own words.
D3	Step 3: Show—Ask students to construct a picture, symbol, or graphic representation of the term.
D1 D2	Step 4: Discuss—Engage students periodically in structured vocabulary discussions that help them add to their knowledge of the terms in their vocabulary

	notebooks.
D1,D2,D3	Step 5: Refine and reflect—Periodically ask students to return to their notebooks to discuss and refine entries.
D1,D2,D3	Step 6: Apply in Learning Games—Involve students periodically in games that allow them to play with terms.

Step 3: Record the instructional steps using the supplied template at LMQ5

LMQ6. Who will do what to support the teaching strategy?

Human / Support Resources

LMQ6 is about marshalling various people and learning systems to assist in the execution of the plan. LMQ6 is a realisation that the classroom teacher is not the only teacher in a contemporary student's life and that many agents such as teacher aides, sporting coaches, experts in the field, grandparents, parents, technology-based learning programs, the Internet, social organisations etc. can be enlisted as part of the overall learning strategy to deliver on the defined learning outcomes. LMQ6 seeks to de-privatise teaching by encouraging teachers to work together and to utilise available others. LMQ6 enables the teacher to strategically move from the age related cohorts to student needs-based cohorts where groups of teachers and para-professionals are enlisted to harness talents and expertise. LMQ6, together with LMQ4, enables the teacher to create at standard and special consideration student profiles and to organise them into manageable learning situations for delivery by others or other arrangements

---
The Steps to Follow

Step 1: Identify the people and 'support' systems' who/ that are able to constitute a teaching team/ system.

Step 2: **Record the identified member of a learning team together with their role and function in the lesson (or series of lessons).**

LMQ7. How will I check that students have achieved the defined learning outcomes?

Assessment

LMQ7 is a focus upon identifying evidence that when collected, is to be used to ascertain whether the learning outcomes (from LMQ2) have been achieved. It is called "assessment". LMQ7 is a direct correlate to that of LMQ2 and is used to ascertain the extent of student learning and by association to confirm that LMQ5 strategies have been successful. This means the teacher must choose assessment strategies so that they reveal the extent of achievement with respect to the defined learning outcomes (LMQ2).

The Steps to Follow

Step 1: **Revise the learning outcomes for the classroom curriculum from LMQ2.**

Step 2: **Identify assessment tasks that *best fit* the defined learning outcomes and the knowledge components of a planned curriculum.**

NOTE: the 'key verb' that constitutes each instructional learning outcome is the reference point for a best fit assessment task e.g. Explain the meaning of key terms = an assessment where the student has to 'explain' key terms

Step 3: Decide how you will ensure reliability, validity and fairness in assessment tasks.

Step 4: Record findings for LMQ 7 as a series of assessment strategies linked to each learning outcome.

LMQ8. How will I report student progress?
Reporting

LMQ8 is about informing stakeholders about student progress. LMQ8 is a planning of pro-formas and processes that are to be used to inform the student and key stakeholders, including the parents/caregivers and the wider community about learning progress. This stage of the LMP deals primarily with the extent to which learning outcomes (LMQ2) have been achieved, and from which the next phase in the classroom curriculum will develop. *This is an opportunity to engage the student and other members of the teaching team in dialogue about each student's progress.* This question is also about formally reporting the student's progress against the yardstick of the planned and agreed learning outcomes (from LMQ2). Data from LMQ7 strategies informs the compilation of LMQ8 information.

The Steps to Follow

Step 1: Identify who the stakeholders are for reporting

Step 2: Reflect on the actual learning outcomes (LMQ2) and the context of the classroom curriculum (LMQ5) and develop a reporting framework that best fits.

NOTE: the criteria assigned to assessments and/or the benchmarks and indicators that are included in each syllabus is a good framework to use.

Step 3: Identify the evidence (LMQ7) that you will use to strengthen your report.

Step 4: **Record strategies**

For more information about assessment and reporting see Lynch, D. and Smith, R. (2012) *Assessing and Reporting the Classroom Curriculum in the Knowledge Age*. Primrose Hall: London.

Summary

This chapter has explained a curriculum development model that identifies what needs to be in the classroom curriculum development process with emphasis on the evidence-based teaching strategies that fit. The process is intended to make explicit what's required for the 'outstanding lesson'. Our point is that while teacher creativity is important in the development of teaching strategies, it is not sufficient if the agenda is for *all students* to make the required learning gains. The Learning Management Design Process enables the teacher to sequentially factor and undertake inquiry into the key elements required of the successful lesson and present them in a teaching ready format.

Appendix 1: Learning Management Plan Template

Learning Management Plan for:	(5) What are my teaching strategies?			
(1) What have my students achieved to date?	Lesson	Outcome focus (LMQ2)	Lessons — What is to be taught? What are the Sequential Strategies	Time Frame (LMQ4)
(2) What do I aim to achieve in my students?	1		Step 1: Step 2: Step 3:	
SLO:	2		Step 1: Step 2: Step 3:	
My students will be able to	3		Step 1: Step 2: Step 3:	
	4		Step 1: Step 2: Step 3:	
	5		Step 1: Step 2: Step 3:	
	(6) Who will do what to support my teaching strategies?			

(3) How do my students best learn?

Best practice:

Attitudes and Perceptions

Habits of Mind

Learner Peculiarities

(4) What resources do I have at my disposal?

(7) How will I check to see my students have achieved the defined learning outcomes?

Learning Outcomes (form LMQ2)	Evidence Required	Assessment Strategy	Type Formative / summative	When?
Declarative Knowledge				
Procedural Knowledge				

(8) How will I report student progress?

Learning Outcomes (form LMQ2)	Reporting Strategy	Type Formative / summative	When?

9. Towards a Teaching Performance Culture

David Lynch and Jake Madden

The concept of 'feedback' is intrinsically intertwined in the process of coaching and mentoring in that it is information about how well one is doing in their efforts to achieve a particular professional goal. In this chapter we further examine the concept of feedback as the central premise of a teaching performance culture. The chapter has been designed to provide an understanding of what is meant and thus required for the creation of this teaching performance culture and presents a model for achieving it.

In Chapters 4 and 5 we introduced and explored the concepts of coaching, mentoring and feedback. We argue in these Chapters that these concepts, when transacted as an inter-related set of enduring and embedded processes within the school, come to represent a focused approach to improving a teacher's teaching. This approach we further argue also provides a central mechanism through which the teach**ing** performance of each teacher can be assessed and importantly where a strategy for improvement can be planned and enacted.

In this chapter we further examine the concept of feedback as the central premise of a teaching performance culture. More specifically we examine what is meant and thus required for the creation of this teaching performance culture and present a model for achieving it. Before attending to these matters we first visit the concept of feedback for key points of reference.

Feedback

'Feedback' can be described as being intrinsically intertwined in the process of coaching and mentoring in that it is information about how well one is doing in their efforts to achieve a particular professional goal. Or as Hattie and Timperley (2007, p.81) state,

> "...feedback is conceptualized as information provided by an agent (e.g., teacher, peer, book, parent, self, experience) regarding aspects of one's performance or understanding. A teacher or parent can provide corrective information, a peer can provide an alternative strategy, a book can provide information to clarify ideas, a parent can provide encouragement, and a learner can look up the answer to evaluate the correctness of a response. **Feedback thus is a 'consequence' of performance.** (Bold added)

In Chapters 4 and 5, we explained how the concept of feedback creates a framework in which poor teaching performance can be identified and when coupled to a coaching and mentoring regime, an environment and structure to enact teaching improvement. Wiggins (2012) describes effective feedback as having seven attributes and thus provides us with a framework in which to provide effective feedback to teachers on their teaching performance. Wiggins (2012) argues that effective feedback must be:

- Goal-Referenced
- Tangible and Transparent
- Actionable
- User-Friendly
- Timely
- Ongoing

- Consistent

As was outlined in Chapter 1, the aim in compiling this book is to explain what is required for creating the outstanding school. In subsequent chapters the centrality and importance of each teacher's teaching in the school was identified as the key ingredient. To this end feedback comes to represent a key mechanism for teachers to know how well they are personally performing towards a focal goal.

Effective Teaching

We've described feedback as information to the teacher on their performance as a teacher. In the bigger scheme of things, the sum of each teacher's teaching performance comes to represent the school's capacity for becoming the outstanding school. But missing in our detailing thus far is an elaboration on what is meant by effective teaching. Put another way, what do we want teachers to do so we can create this outstanding school?

We can take reference from Coe, et al. (2014, p.1) who define effective teaching "as that which leads to improved student achievement using outcomes that matter to their future success". Their key point is that "the research keeps coming back to this critical point: student progress is the yardstick by which teacher quality should be assessed". Further, Coe et al. (2014, p.1) provide advice in that "ultimately, for a judgement about whether teaching is effective, to be seen as trustworthy, it must be checked against the progress being made by students".

We are further assisted in understanding the attributes of effective teaching once again by Coe et, al. (2014), who in Table 1, provide us with 6 effective teaching attributes and their research-based impact on student outcomes, for points of reference.

Effective Teaching Component	Key Attribute	Effect Factor
Quality of instruction	Includes elements such as effective questioning and use of assessment by teachers. Specific practices, like reviewing previous learning, providing model responses for students, giving adequate time for practice to embed skills securely Executive Summary 3 and progressively introducing new learning (scaffolding) are also elements of high quality instruction.	**Strong evidence** of impact on student outcomes
(Pedagogical) content knowledge	The most effective teachers have deep knowledge of the subjects they teach, and when teachers' knowledge falls below a certain level it is a significant impediment to students' learning. As well as a strong understanding of the material being taught, teachers must also understand the ways students think about the content, be able to evaluate the thinking behind students' own methods, and identify students' common misconceptions.	**Strong evidence** of impact on student outcomes
Classroom climate	Covers quality of interactions between teachers and students, and teacher expectations: the need to create a classroom that is constantly demanding more, but still recognising students' self-worth. It also involves attributing student success to effort rather than ability and valuing resilience to failure (grit).	**Moderate evidence** of impact on student outcomes
Classroom management	A teacher's abilities to make efficient use of lesson time, to coordinate classroom resources and space, and to manage students' behaviour with clear rules that are consistently enforced, are all relevant to maximising the learning that can take place. These environmental factors are necessary for good learning rather than its direct components.	**Moderate evidence** of impact on student outcomes
Teacher beliefs	Why teachers adopt particular practices, the purposes they aim to achieve, their theories about what learning is and how it happens and their conceptual models of the nature	**Some evidence** of impact on student outcomes

	and role of teaching in the learning process all seem to be important	
Professional behaviours	Behaviours exhibited by teachers such as reflecting on and developing professional practice, participation in professional development, supporting colleagues, and liaising and communicating with parents.	**Some evidence** of impact on student outcomes

Table 1: The Components of Effective Teaching and their Research based Effect Factor (Coe, et al, 2014, pp. 1-2)

What Coe et al. (2014) through Table 1 effectively provides is an outlining of what a teacher needs to do to be effective --- that is achieve defined learning outcomes in each student --- and by direct association these Table 1 elements become potential reference points, for what we as coaches and mentors have to provide feedback on and thus instigate associated interventions.

The Teaching Performance Culture

In previous published works Smith and Lynch (2010; 2006) and Lynch (2012) provide commentary on the need for a fundamental shift in the way teachers conceptualise and then go about their business as teachers. While their commentaries focus on the deficiencies of initial teacher education, their work does provide us with an insight into what can be figuratively described as the acceptance of a 'normal distribution' in classrooms. While we don't seek to discuss the fundamentals of what a normal distribution is --- i.e. the bell curve --- and how it comes to be represented statistically, the point we want to make is that the 'bell curve' has become a euphemism for what is acceptable student performance in a classroom for a student cohort year-on-in. In more simple terms there's an apparent acceptance in traditional teaching ranks that in any given classroom you will have the proverbial 'slow kids', 'smart kids' and a lot of kids in the middle: i.e. the bell curve. The point we make, and we refer to Hattie (2012, 2011, 2009) to make this point, is that teachers can make a difference in student learning performance and thus impact the distribution of learning performance in their classrooms. Hattie (2009) provides further advice in this matter in that he argues a >0.4 teaching effect size [37] is the goal for teachers if they are to ensure their students are not going backwards. To this end we highlight the need for student performance data and comparisons to be made of same over time. This data in turn forms the backbone of teaching 'feedback'. The target growth in student learning according to Hattie (2009) is >0.4 effect size and we can thus use this criterion to judge how well teachers are performing. Returning the premise of the 'bell curve' our point is that if we are to create the outstanding school then every teacher in the school must see promise in their capacities to improve their teaching performance and thus be focused to achieving this Hattie (2009) performance criterion. Taken together we create the outstanding school for every student's benefit.

Summary and Conclusion

In previous chapters we have detailed the coupling of coaching and mentoring to feedback and in doing so conceptualised a mechanism for developing the effective teacher. Feedback in this context comes to represent a detailing of how well a teacher is performing, a stating of what they need to focus on to improve and is always referenced to a particular goal. We've argued that the strategy for a school wanting to become outstanding is to ensure that every student makes learning gains. Hattie's (2009) effect size criterion provides the school with a focus to build and defend the constituents of what 'acceptable' teaching performance is and from this a strategy can be developed to make same outstanding.

---

[37] An effect-size provides a common expression of the magnitude of study outcomes for all types of outcome variables, such as school achievement.

Taken together these elements and those outlined in previous chapters come to represent a cohesive framework for achieving a teaching performance culture focused on becoming outstanding.

10. TEACHERS AS RESEARCHERS

David Lynch and Jake Madden

> In this chapter we further the idea of a teaching performance school improvement strategy. The 'teacher as researcher' idea comes to represent a strategy for enabling teachers to better understand their profession, to make informed teaching decisions and to contribute to the growth of their profession by making valid contributions to it.

To this point in the book, a series of chapters have been presented which focus the reader to a key aspect of creating the outstanding school. Missing thus far is the role teachers play in generating and harnessing research for teaching effect. While this notion is implicit in the 'research and evidence based practice' lines throughout the book, in this chapter we focus to the concept more specifically. We effectively outline and then explore what occurs when teachers begin to inquire into their own teaching practice and that of their colleagues and then publish the results for others and self to reference. We term this arrangement the 'teacher as researcher'.

From Compliant Consumers of Knowledge to Active Creators

The history of teaching and its counterpart teacher education is enmeshed in a legacy triggered by the advent of the 1700's 'Industrial Revolution'. The Industrial Revolution represented a major upheaval of the society of the time, but it occurred over many centuries. This time factor is important because it enabled the establishment of strong and embedded traditions within our schools and which this book is focused on resolving. As the government and industries of the time sought to come to terms with the radical changes that the Industrial Revolution created, schooling systems were established to prepare the masses for a new work and home life (Lynch, 2012).

The predictability and uniformity of the Industrial Revolution required that emerging new knowledge be transmitted efficiently, but in 'one way' --- from expert to novice --- and in a context of strict regimentation and conformity. This circumstance was a forerunner to the society in which students were to enter as adults. Hence the traditions of schooling --- with students lined up ready to receive knowledge, teacher centred activities, salutations, hierarchies, strict behavior norms, grade levels, parades, and the like --- came into being.

Students who showed capacity for further learning continued up a hierarchy of 'grades' while the less able 'dropped out' and commenced work: be it through unskilled work, apprenticeship or on the job training. Because of a lack of viable technology on communication and transport fronts, societies of the time were largely insular and thus not exposed to outside forces for change. Established societal processes and ways of doing things thus stayed largely unchanged for nearly 200+ years. This is the case for schools.

'Jobs for life' became the norm and society established itself around yet more norms on which many of the current traditions in society have their origins (e.g. the 5 day, 9 to 5 Monday to Friday working week, penalty rates, award rates for pay, long-service leave, collective bargaining, etc.) . The schooling syllabus reflected this circumstance. The direct trajectory of students through schools and into a 'place in work' --- albeit into differing 'levels' of the workforce and with limited potentials for career variety --- required teachers to maintain a strict sense of 'sameness' in their approaches for each student cohort. There was no need for research into education, nor was there any point, in fact it was a detriment to this well-oiled schooling system, for teachers to work outside what became established teaching practice norms. All in all this circumstance became known as 'schooling' and the political language set of the time put a premium on its importance over 'teaching'.

But all this came under pressure as society entered the 1990s. The Knowledge Economy made its entrance and the fundamentals on which schools had previously existed began to become shaky.

Underpinning the Knowledge Economy is a set of interwoven technological advancements that are the result of human brainpower and networked ideas. These advancements are stimulated by a consumer driven market and their seemingly insatiable desire for 'a better', more convenient, social and entertaining existence. In this 'new world' the consumer seeks a capacity to 'delegate' the drudgery of everyday life to a gadget, be connected and up-to-date on a 24/7 basis, but only on topics and with people of interest, and have their next 'want' satisfied in new and unique ways and often with the expectations that it will all be for free and immediate.

On another plane, this circumstance of innovation and creativity is coalescing around concepts such as automation and interconnectivity creating still larger bodies of knowledge and technological potentials, each waiting to be released as the next big thing. On the 'education front' this new era has unearthed sophisticated understandings about how people learn and how teachers can best teach and has provided teachers (and others) with access to data sources that enable them to conduct their own inquiry.

In simple terms we now know that one's success at school can be radically enhanced by the 'expert and competent' teacher (Hattie,

2009; 2012) and a capacity to engage in research is a highly potent value-add for professional practice in a knowledge based economy.

For teachers and schooling systems alike this new societal context is both an opportunity and a challenge. It's an opportunity because technological advancement offers alternatives to the 'chalk and talk' classroom-learning paradigm of the past, while generating new understandings about how people learn. It is also creating, and in some cases demanding, that teachers become creators and contributors to professional knowledge and understanding: not as a work 'add on' but as a key component of professional life in a Knowledge Economy circumstance. A challenge because this new society represents a fundamental disconnect from the world in which our aging teacher workforce was initially trained and a distinct contrast to the rigid structures of schooling and its Industrial Era hallmarks. But to chart a new course means people have to contribute to its research.

The Advent of Teacher Inquiry

As we indicated in an earlier section, a distinct feature of the Knowledge Economy is the notion of constant change. This is a contrast to the previous industrial era in which schools were created. This change is not isolated to just industry and other means of production, but by direct associations and entanglement, encumbered to every part of modern society. While the premise of what this change means for teachers is complex and largely enmeshed in an amalgam of what was outlined in previous chapters, the key points we seek to highlight is that teaching is now a highly sophisticated affair.

Further, teachers must now also become innovators, problem solvers, networkers, knowledge creators and agents for change. To get at the heart of this new phenomenon and to enact a mindset to enable this new approach, we argue that teachers must embed themselves in a culture of inquiry, or as we like to call it, become teachers as researchers.

The Culture of Teaching Inquiry

In Chapter 8 we introduced the concept of the Learning Management Design Process. This teaching design process with its 8 questions comes to represent this culture of inquiry at the curriculum planning level. No longer are teachers able to strictly follow long established chalk and talk and text-book based norms and satisfy themselves with 'bell curve' or flat-lining student results. Society requires all members to be highly educated and adaptable to the complexities that the Knowledge Economy now generates and the inherent ongoing changes it manifests. Taken together teachers have to chart new learning courses, reflect on outcomes and strive for better results. Not for the sake of efficiencies but to enable future generations to find their place in a complex changing society. But what does this culture of inquiry actually mean?

In short, this culture of inquiry requires the teacher to begin to ask 'why' and 'why not' type questions and seek answers to them. To no longer just accept what 'has been' or 'what just results' but engage in their own school-based research: analyse and interpret the results of their endeavours, couple same to the context of their school and its student cohorts and then use findings to explore alternatives and test propositions as the basis of their decision-making. All-in-all this process can be described as 'action research'.

According to Reason and Bradbury (2006) there is no 'short answer' to explain the complexities of action research. They articulate action research as:

> "A participatory, democratic process concerned with developing practical knowing in the pursuit of worthwhile human purposes, grounded in a participatory worldview which we believe is emerging at this historical moment" (Reason & Bradbury, 2006, p. 2)

The primary purpose of action research is to produce knowledge that is useful to people in the everyday nature of their lives. Three particular characteristics of action research are that:

- it arises from practical questions;
- is participatory in nature; and
- it's validity is strengthened through peer examination and discussion. (Bartlett & Burton, 2006, p. 401)

It is thought that Kurt Lewin conceived the concept of action research as a cyclic phenomenon (Dickens & Watkins, 1999) built on the traditional scientific paradigm with the results being expressed in 'if/so' propositions.

Stringer (1996) offers an ecological lens to view action research. In short it refers to a three step method as explained:

1. Look: Gather information related to what is most valued to the goals or the work of the school.
2. Think: After identifying relevant assumptions and expectations, analyze/interpret this information to evaluate possible antecedents, cultural and theoretical assumptions, ideologies, influences, consequences and potential actions.
3. Act: This part of the cycle often involves posing new questions that lead to further inquiry. (Stringer, 1999)

This premise is explored in greater depth by Freebody (2003) who views action research as a 'deliberate' rather than a purely exploratory entry into a naturally occurring educational setting. That is, it is a planned and self-consciously focused examination of changing practice and has a number of components. For Freebody, a key characteristic of action research is that it is a solution-oriented investigation aimed explicitly at understanding and solving particular problems rather than simply documenting their instances, character or consequences.

Freebody (2003) has presented a six step action research process:

1. Selecting a focus
2. Collection of data
3. Analyse, document and review data
4. Develop analytical categories
5. Organise data and its interpretations
6. Take action and repeat cycle.
   (Freebody, 2003)

This action research can either be conducted by a group or personally owned. However, the emphasis here is on the importance of the researchers' role in defining the problem, what counts as solutions, and what form the reporting of the project will take.

The central component of this action research is the 'loop' factor (step 6, previously). This takes the form of a series of iterations on and around the problem, its documentation and theorization, and the analyses that are used to display how it has been redefined and solved. For some, these iterations are referred to as spirals (Stringer, 1999) but are more commonly known as the Action Research cycle. This cyclic feature of Action Research is taken to be central to its core emphasis on the documented improvement of practice.

Stringer (2004) elaborated on his "Look, Think, Act" model following a more qualitative interpretive research design as outlined in Figure 1.

1. **Research Design** – initiating a study

2. **Data Gathering** – Capturing stakeholder experiences and perspectives

3. **Data Analysis** – Capturing identifying key features of experience

4. **Communication** – Writing reports

5. **Action** – Creating solutions

Figure 1: Stringer's Qualitative Interpretive Research Design

The 'trying out of ideas' (or creating solutions) is not undertaken solely for the purposes of re-theorizing educational practice, or adding to knowledge, but is also aimed at improving educational practice, at the moment it is needed. In that respect, action research is concerned as much with outcomes on the original research as it is with generalizations to other research or leading to theoretical refinement (Reason & Bradbury, 2006).

Action research is seen as a collaborative enterprise as it provides opportunities for colleagues to share, discuss and debate aspects of their practice with the aim of fostering school improvement and development. This involves responsible 'sense-making' or interpretation of data collected from within the field of researchers' own practice.

One way forward for the classroom teacher is to become a researcher. Lawrence Stenhouse, in his book, "An Introduction to Curriculum Research and Development (1975) popularised the term "Teacher as Researcher". The purpose of Teacher as Researcher is simply to enhance their own (or that of their colleagues) teaching ability. It's a systematic reflection on their teaching practices with the sole aim of personal improvement.

For the teacher researcher, the purpose of school based research is fourfold:

- <u>Address the gaps in the current knowledge</u> by allowing teachers to investigating voids in their (own) teaching practice
- <u>Expand the knowledge</u> of teachers
- <u>Test the knowledge</u> already known about teaching and to apply it to new circumstances or with different participants
- <u>Add voices</u> not yet heard to the research knowledge (Creswell, 2002)

In the mid to late 1970's, 'Teacher as Researcher' was generally an individualized notion, looking at a teacher's practice as an isolated activity within the school, and even isolated from colleagues. However, today we see the focus of classroom research as part of the whole school and even, at times, at the system level. Teacher research also captures student learning and development using data that focuses on using student voices.

A consequence of teachers undertaking action research (inside their classroom) is that it becomes more meaningful (and personal) to the classroom practitioner, promotes the voice of the teacher and highlights their professional role. Teacher researchers become the creators of knowledge. Schools are beginning to take an interest into this research as a means to inform their decision-making across many dimensions of school life. While school improvement remains the major basis for schools focusing on 'in school' research, other areas are becoming more prominent. These include workplace health and safety, physical learning environments and even issues around professional development.

The move away from university based research that guides the theory enacted in schools has been accentuated by the need for teachers to be more hands on in determining student learning needs (Babkie & Provost, 2004). When discussing teachers as researchers, the focus is not on an experimental approach to teaching, but rather a practical means to improving teaching and learning.

As no two classrooms are alike the need for the teacher to be able to tailor the curriculum to the needs of each student becomes more apparent. The teacher must be able to rely on his/her knowledge through careful systematic observation guided by an understanding of various hypotheses to each context faced.

Conclusion

Research by teachers as part of their day to day teaching life is not only an effective way of addressing and meeting the learning needs of students but also an effective means for focusing on improved teacher practice (Mills, 2000). It builds teacher capacity, sharpens leadership skills and supports the foundations of current educational agendas. In supporting teachers as researchers, as a means of raising student achievement and improving teacher practice, the hidden consequence is the promotion of 'distributed leadership' (e.g. Gronn, 2000; Spillane 2005) across the school.

The idea of action research means educational problems and issues can be identified and investigated where the action is. That is, at the classroom and school level. By integrating research into these settings and engaging those who work at this level in research activities, findings can be applied immediately and problems solved more quickly.

Action research is also a model of professional development in which teachers study 'topics' or 'phenomena' related to their own teaching practice --- to think and reflect upon findings and locate new learnings. In effect it comes to represent a process that allows teachers to learn about their own instructional practices and to know what to focus on so as to improve their student learning.

Much of what occurs in education is the result of taken-for-granted routines, ideologies, top down mandates and untested assumptions and beliefs. However, schools are now in an age where knowledge is 'king' and the teacher as researcher premise is a vehicle to positioning teachers as 21st Century knowledge practitioners.

11. Building the Outstanding School: A Principal's insights into what it all means.

Helen Spiers

> This chapter explores the commencement of the Collaborative Teacher Learning Model (CTLM) by a Darwin-based independent 'Foundation to Year 12' school. In effect the school aims to build on findings as outlined in this book for direct school-wide improvement. This chapter provides an insight into the CTLM and how it is being implemented in a school with many inherent challenges.

This chapter is a case study into Kormilda College where the *Collaborative Teacher Learning Model* (CTLM) is being implemented. The CTLM was detailed in Chapter 2 and 5. In effect the school aims to build on findings as outlined in this book on its journey to becoming the outstanding school. More specifically the chapter provides an insight into the CTLM and how I as a principal have used it to focus my school toward achieving outstanding school results. What makes the chapter interesting is that the CTLM is being implemented in a school with many inherent challenges. Before commencing with this case, I briefly provide an insight into the education environment in which Kormilda College operates.

Education in the Northern Territory

The provision of school-aged education in the Northern Territory of Australia (NT), one of two Territories and seven States in Australia that make up this continent, occurs within a unique context and includes a diverse student group. The Northern Territory has a small diverse population of 244,000 people spread over an area of 1.3 million square kilometres. The NT's capital city, Darwin, is the second fastest growing city in Australia, with 136,000 people, compared to Dubai, a city with a daytime population of over 3 million within the federation of the United Arab Emirates, which covers 83,000 square kilometres (United Arab Emirates, 2014, October 13).

All schools in the Northern Territory reflect the culturally and linguistically diverse backgrounds of the population of the Top End of Australia with both established and newly arrived families from the Asia-Pacific areas as well as Europe. The NT population also includes 30% of people identifying as Indigenous Australians, the majority of whom reside in very remote locations (Wilson, 2014, p.15). However, the participation rates of Indigenous Australian people from remote communities in senior levels of schooling remains low. Only 29% of the NT Indigenous population attends school beyond Year 10 and the average attendance of senior school students in very remote schools is 30% (Ibid, p. 137).

School-aged education is delivered in Darwin through thirty State or Government-funded Primary Schools, eight State secondary schools, two special schools for disabled students, nine Catholic schools and nine Independent schools.

One of the Independent schools in Darwin, situated about 12 kms from the Central Business District, is Kormilda College, a provider of Foundation (five year olds) to Year 12 school-aged education. In the Northern Territory (NT), Kormilda College is unique in that it is an International Baccalaureate (IB) school, the only Northern Territory school offering the International Baccalaureate suite of programmes at both Middle School and Senior School. Due to the recent opening of a Primary School on site, the College is shortly due to commence the accreditation process to be able to also offer the International Baccalaureate Primary Years Programme (PYP). Overall, the school population is 650 students and climbing, with two-thirds of these students residing in the Darwin urban and rural areas and attending as Day students. The remaining one third of the student population identify as Indigenous and attend as Boarding students.

This leads to another aspect to Kormilda's uniqueness. For over twenty years Kormilda College, a jointly owned Anglican and Uniting Church Day and Boarding school, has provided opportunities for Indigenous students from remote communities throughout Northern, Central and Western Australia to participate in a high quality secondary education.

These Indigenous students enrol at Kormilda College from forty different remote communities bringing with them a variety of cultural practices and sensitivities. These students are full-time boarders at the school during term times and during school hours there is the potential for these students to study alongside Indigenous and non-Indigenous Day students. In effect the multitude of educational offerings should facilitate a joint learning experience and produce benefits to both cohorts of students (Rhodes & Spiers, 2014, p. 4). Theoretically this is one model of inclusive education, creating an environment in which every student has the opportunity to flourish.

However, the reality of the situation produces a very different picture than what is envisaged by the underlying philosophy of the College. 'School Readiness' of students arriving from remote communities is low, that is their ability to understand and cope with the expectations of attending a school based on a very Western system of education. By this is meant an education aimed at creating a pathway to social mobility, offering great economic returns and alleviating social disadvantage. However it can also mean that this form of education does not allow, or can manage the practicalities, for learning to be delivered in first language and is not inclusive of social, cultural and economic values held by the students. At its worst, education can be a tool of acculturation and assimilation for remote Aboriginal people. Education can usurp local social structures, cause deep intergenerational divisions and not be connected to the reality of a student's daily life in remote community. The result is that education can seem utterly pointless, leading to disengagement (Fogarty, 2012).

Low literacy levels amongst the Aboriginal students cohort at urban schools in Darwin and frequently low levels of school readiness, as mentioned in the previous paragraph, means that it is virtually impossible for very many Aboriginal students to study in the same class as non-Aboriginal or urban Aboriginal students. Recent National Assessment Program – Literacy and Numeracy (NAPLAN) data certainly demonstrates a clear and large "gap" between these cohorts, ranging from 36-60% gap in educational attainment. The recent NT Indigenous Education Review (Wilson, 2014, p. 54) notes that the largest gaps are for the very remote Indigenous student cohort: "Here the variations are dramatically negative". At Year 5, remote students are two years behind in writing skills compared to the rest of Australia and at Year 9 they are five years behind.

A recent publication (AIEF, 2015, p. 10) stated that many Australian leaders are disturbed by the crisis in Aboriginal education and the risk of losing an entire generation of Aboriginal children. The result is a general high level of disengagement from formal education within the Aboriginal cohort across Australia and perceived disappointment in the non-Aboriginal student group attending a school such as Kormilda College because expectations of cross-cultural experiences cannot be met.

As a result of the complexity surrounding Aboriginal Education in Australia, Aboriginal people in remote Australia face a great and deep dilemma in engaging with the current education system. However, Kormilda College has a history of knowing and implementing what works. Firstly, subject content must be engaging, accessible and culturally responsive with a school culture that supports this and builds on high expectations for all students. Secondly, within the practices of the school Aboriginal and Torres Strait Islander students need to be empowered, supported and engaged to enhance their own learning capacity, while teacher capacity is strengthened around cultural competency (Fogarty, 2012). Thirdly, a coherent and localised approach to evidence-based literacy and numeracy teaching is essential whilst also appreciating, and implementing strategies to ensure, that a profound understanding of the importance of school-community partnerships remains a school strategic focus.

The College is now commencing the journey of the above-mentioned approach to evidence-based literacy teaching and this paper will describe the challenges and successes so far.

Challenges at Kormilda College

The challenges described above continue to remain a daily focus of staff at Kormilda College as the operational concerns of the whole college are managed. Due to the academic diversity of students at the college, from Aboriginal students with low literacy to those studying highly academic International Baccalaureate programmes, plus the social diversity of one third of the student cohort strongly connected to Aboriginal cultural practices and two thirds living an urban, middle class lifestyle with various levels of connection with a formal religion, the day to day operational matters can easily distract teachers and management from the core responsibility of a school.

A school's core business is to educate the attending students and the focus of management must be to ensure effective teaching and learning is taking place within the school. But within a complex school with a diverse range of students and levels of literacy a multi-faceted approach is required. Yet there is a general recognition and acceptance that everybody is continually learning when it comes to Aboriginal education and nobody would claim to have mastered it (AIEF, 2015, p.10). Therefore the possibility exists that some teachers will have high expectations of their students whilst others may feel compassion and empathy for the plight of students from a different cultural background and, as a result, not have such high expectations as are required for adequate advancement in learning over time. As a result of acknowledging the complexities of the student learning environment at Kormilda College, senior management staff decided to examine the data more closely and collaborate with external educational academics who could potentially assist them to move the school from a good school with satisfactory results across all student groups to a great school with outstanding student satisfaction and engagement.

Evidence and a Way forward

With all of these challenges, real and perceived, it was timely to see if Kormilda College has been able to overcome these social and cultural challenges and become a great school, matching its aspirations. As mentioned in the introduction, this journey for Kormilda College has only just begun. The last four decades of research in education have produced a treasure trove of information about how students learn, how effective schools and effective teachers work, what teachers need to do their work well, and what good leadership looks like in schools and districts. The education profession knows a lot about what works, or stated more accurately, what is *most likely* to work (Marzano, 2003). When senior management at Kormilda College examined the data available to them it was clear that the collection was extensive. Various pieces of data are collected from each student upon arrival at Kormilda College. In most instances the usual form is previous reports and teacher or community references. In terms of the Aboriginal students, whilst they are expected to have attended school during the previous six months, documentation may be unavailable so academic screening occurs upon their arrival at Kormilda. This is repeated at the commencement of each subsequent semester. All students in the college undertake an Australian Council of Educational Research (ACER) standardised test at the commencement of each year to attempt to measure gaps in learning. As mentioned earlier, should student be in Years 3, 5, 7 and 9 then they also participate in the National Assessment Program – Literacy and Numeracy (NAPLAN). Australian student results in these regular assessments over the past five years indicates a wide spread of literacy and numeracy levels. At Year 9 NAPLAN testing over the past three years, Aboriginal students at Kormilda College have consistently displayed results whereby 53% of the Aboriginal student cohort for that year are at or above benchmark attainment in Numeracy, 41% at or above benchmark in Writing, 35% at or above benchmark in Reading and 29% at or above benchmark in Grammar and Punctuation. Whilst this is an improvement on their results upon commencement at Kormilda College in Year 7, two years earlier, there is little evidence to be able to gauge just what this means in terms of the actual learning that has taken place. Statistically, attendance by an Aboriginal student at Kormilda College over a lengthy period of time, possibly 3-5 years, does appear to improve results by an average of 15% each year. The result of such data examination resulted in a focus by senior management on the most effective strategies, including a culturally appropriate focus on teaching and learning.

If a close study is made of specific individual students over a period of several years it can be demonstrated that this level of improvement will mean that by senior school, after potentially six years at Kormilda College, the students will have reached a literacy level at which they are capable academically of completing the NT's Year 12 education certificate, called the Northern Territory

Certificate of Education and Training (NTCET). It is worth noting that the adjective "capable' was used because it is certainly not assured that this will eventuate. It does occur but not concerning all of our potential candidates for completion of Year 12 with regards to our Aboriginal population at school. Senior management considered that this was not the definition of a great school so further improvement in the use of data was considered essential. In summary, considering both NAPLAN and ACER results, Kormilda College could be considered an average to above average school. But this would not be so if the Aboriginal student results were considered on their own as ACER raw data would suggest that these students are still several years behind their non-Aboriginal counterparts in terms of English literacy attainment, even when they reach their final year of schooling. For a great school, this would not be acceptable. More concrete evidence of actual teaching and learning progress needed to be found.

The Research indicates that when teachers develop their own inquiry skills and apply them, it is more likely that there will be sustained improvement in teaching effectiveness (Lynch & Madden, 2015, p. 5). In seeking to develop a deeper understanding of a 'sustained improvement', a line of inquiry was sought by college management into what Hattie (2012, p. 1) meant by the comment that student learning needs to be visible to teachers and teaching needs to be visible to students. The Kormilda College philosophy to review practice and ensure that we were not being side-tracked away from our core business fitted well with Hattie's premise (2012, p. 18) that schools need to retain learning at the forefront and consider teaching primarily in terms of its impact on student learning. That is, learning must be the explicit and transparent goal with both the teacher and student ascertaining whether and to what degree the challenging goal is attained (p. 18). What does matter, says Hattie (2012, p. 18) is that teachers have a mind frame in which they see it as their role to evaluate their effect on learning.

As if on cue for Kormilda College, the CTLM team, led by David Lynch and Jake Madden visited the Northern Territory and proposed a long term research project as an extension of their 5 year pilot project, as outlined in Chapter 2. The research planned to evaluate the effect of introducing a routine of coaching, mentoring and feedback (CMF) into the cycle of teaching and learning with the aim of measuring its effect on student learning. In effect, this meant that if we supported this initiative we could be part of an extended program of school improvement. This arrangement is known in the literature as the *Collaborative Teacher Learning Model (CTLM)*. As Principal of a school wanting to create an outstanding school this offer was too good to pass up. The twenty-first century context was demanding that student learning would become Kormilda's focus and staff would professional grow and support each other. To create school-wide ownership and to focus the CTLM into the school we termed our version of the project, the Cross Curricular Literacy Project.

Pathway for Change Identified

At the outset, as Lynch & Madden (2005) noted (p.5), the CMF regime is the over-arching mechanism for school improvement through which the teaching performance of each teacher is assessed through year level data collection, the results of which assist in the development of strategies to improve individual student learning. In line with Kormilda College practice that students are individually academically tracked, this way forward was morally the right way to go but practically, it was perplexing for a Principal in only her second year at the helm. So, in conjunction with the team from Southern Cross University and Kormilda's senior management team, a way forward was devised but it had to be systematic as to include all staff and ensure that parents understood the change in practices.

Firstly the Principal had to be fully committed to the project. This fitted in well with the research on leadership. The two greatest failures of leaders, according to Michael Fullan (2008, p.6), are "indecisiveness in times of urgent need for action and dead certainty that they are right in times of complexity". Lynch & Madden (2015) note a 0.25 correlation between a Principal's leadership and student achievement (p.4). If focused, the Head's leadership could potentially increase student achievement by 22% higher than the starting percentile. In Pearson's r Correlation terms this is a weak but positive relationship between Principal and student achievement so this was a positive step to consider. The Principal also consulted with the College Board of Directors and received overwhelming support as the expectations were in line with the College's Strategic directions. Potentially, with the additional support of the College Board, consisting of Directors from both the Anglican and the Uniting Churches, this 0.25 correlation may be lifted into the realms of 0.30 and above, an improved level of positive relationship.

The next step was to involve members of senior management. This pivotal group needed to also be supportive of the research as it was in their various roles across the college that the word would spread and staff would begin to take leadership roles. It was agreed that the focus for the Building an Outstanding School would commence with improving Literacy across the college, due mostly to our ongoing commitment to improving English literacy with our Aboriginal students and the fact that our school was adequately supported by teachers with the necessary qualifications. It was always intended that a focus on Numeracy would follow six months later. Additionally, a general conversation with parents had to occur at the earliest convenience so the forum of the Parents Consultative Group meeting, usually held each term, was determined as the appropriate time to share this exciting new venture with parents and friends of Kormilda College. Again, because of the potential to improve the learning of all students and the professionalism of all staff, the Principal received positive support.

Once senior management staff were ready to embrace this initiative, the process of collaborating and communicating with staff began in earnest with Professor Lynch speaking with academic staff at a staff meeting with the Principal present to show solidarity and support. Having an external expert to speak with staff was essential as this demonstrated rigour and commitment. At a later date, a Principal of a school previously involved in the pilot program spoke with senior managers and pivotal staff and this also was welcomed. By now staff became excited. It made sense. They now understood the reason behind a whole of school data collection (ACER) and also appreciated that they were the 'experts' at student level and were well aware of shortfalls in student knowledge but had not spent the necessary time to date in actually peeling back the layers of academic gaps and delivering appropriate intervention. In small group conversations they acknowledged that there were classes where whole areas of the curriculum were not well known by students.

The benefit of a whole of school approach to teaching and learning improvement through data analysis is that teachers, often in year level clusters, can personally take on the responsibility for improvement of individual students by seeing the data first hand, not just an in-house assessment but a whole of school data collection, and sharing the analysis with colleagues. This is the basis for convincing staff for the need for improvement. After all that is what they are paid to do, no-one else, they are paid to educate and have their students achieve.

Summarising: Principals over past five years have spoken of high expectations. This has not been enough to guarantee explicit and effective learning. Staff have been involved in strategies to improve NAPLAN test results. Again, the analysis of these results have simply not been enough. There is an urgent need for improvement at the coalface, at the teacher level, using easily understood data analysis. The data actually needs to be interpreted at the personal level, the student level, for it to have meaning.

Practice versus Theory

With the pathway to improvement now clear, determining the next step involved the Head of Middle School leading her team of Year-level coordinators and Heads of Department. Staff were supported to find the time to meet as year level groups and develop a common assessment task, focusing on English literacy. In six months' time a similar task will be ready to assess Numeracy standards at year levels. That is our plan. Most staff either teach Literacy or Numeracy based subjects. They were all involved in the lead up to the process although the English Department took a major lead in the development of the assessment task. They wanted to be effective. Those inclined to feel it was an English teacher role were counselled and encouraged. The Principal and Senior Managers ensured that all staff heard the message that their role is to educate and to be effective in that role and that this was what would be measured, not for any punitive purpose but for their increased professionalism and accountability to families and their students.

Commencing Term Three this year all academic staff participated in ensuring that their students completed the writing task that had been set by the English faculty. The topic of conversation moved into use of the term Professional Learning Communities as a way of describing what it was that was happening. Staff were meeting to share their vision for the future of their classroom learning environment and considering strategies across year levels to ensure gaps in student knowledge, when identified, were managed. During this time, staff were also meeting for short periods each week for the overall marking and reviewing of results of the writing task per year levels to establish common gaps in knowledge. Then further meetings were held to collaborate on who would be assigned to teach the students the gaps in their learning.

This is where POIL came into being and became a focus: Planning, Organisation, Instruction and Leadership. Improvement in literacy levels across the school now relied on a formal process of quality planning, every teacher being involved in the organisation of the process, direct and explicit instruction to students once gaps in learning had been identified and strong levels of leadership at a variety of academic or organisational areas across the whole school.

Summarising: The Cross Curricular Literacy Project has two main goals over the next three years:

1. To improve student results in literacy, specifically language conventions, each year. This is measured and analysed by all staff on a regular basis and used to shape teaching pedagogy.
2. Staff are involved in regular and meaningful professional learning communities that provide opportunities for coaching, mentoring and feedback regarding high impact teaching and learning practices.

Sub-goals have been developed for the next two semesters:

Term Three	Develop professional learning communities (create shared vision)
	Change meeting schedule to fit in collaboration times
	Begin writing task
Term Four	Professional learning communities (begin discussions regarding high impact teaching and learning)
	Finish writing task

Challenges to date

Appropriate and relevant communication is always necessary in times of change. Wikoff (2013, para.5) found that "Communication is paramount when trying to raise the level of understanding in your organisation". Consideration has to be given to the communication with parents in terms of what is planned, how it will occur and what will be the benefit to their children and to the college. In our initial forums with parents it was essential that we did not use what would locally be called Education Speak. Another challenge has been teacher involvement and commitment. There are those who have practised teaching for a long time and are not motivated to change. To enthuse, change strategies are used. There are also staff who are new to the profession, who feel overwhelmed with their current commitments, and cannot see their way clear to add anything else on. In empathising with their dilemma, these staff were persuaded that this initiative was not an 'add-on' but an 'instead of'. It was also emphasised that this was an initiative based on staff collaboration within year levels, not a process solely dependent on individuals working alone. Staff were encouraged to work together in planning the writing task, using a common rubric. The process ensured that neophyte staff, that is staff new to the profession, have a more experienced mentor teacher with them through this process. The positives were enthusiastically embraced by many staff because not only did it benefit them professionally but enabled them to align outcomes with current practices on staff appraisal and to update their personal profile.

Summarising: This initiative satisfies an intrinsic motivation to be as professional as a person can be and so in a very short time all staff were embracing the challenge and participating in development and analysing of the writing task.

Anecdotal evidence of change

Outstandingly, the successors to date have been an increase in whole school focus on Literacy across all subject areas. It has always been the focus of staff teaching Kormilda College's Aboriginal students but now it is acknowledged as a focus for the whole school. Anecdotally, there has been increased staff participation in data analysis and data-driven decision-making concerning strategies for student improvement in learning. It is expected that this development of teaching leaders amongst the academic staff and improved capability to use data will be among the results of the Southern Cross University staff survey undertaken mid-year. This survey has been designed to analyse the 'profile' of all staff in the school for education centred changes tracked over time.

The Journey Continues

This is but the beginning of a process of school improvement at Kormilda College by having a whole school approach of focusing on the work of the teacher. Through a coordinated process of 'leadership' and 'data-driven decision making', supported by a 'coaching, mentoring and feedback' regime for measuring the resultant teacher effect on Literacy development, it is expected that all of Kormilda students will benefit. In particular, the remote Aboriginal students boarding at the College will reap the rewards of a visionary university-school partnership. There is no 'one size fits all' solution as Hattie (2012, p. 192) reminds us. The initiative is about recapturing schools in order to optimise and esteem the positive impacts that all teaching staff have on student learning. A cultural shift is occurring at Kormilda College and staff are ready for the challenge. It will be an exciting journey with all students being the winners. In particular, remotely based Aboriginal students will be empowered to become Australia's leaders of tomorrow.

Reference List

Abbott, J. (1999). *Battery hens or free range chickens what kind of education for what kind of world? 21ˢᵗ Learning organisation.* Retrieved from http://www.21learn.org/archive/battery-hens-or-free-range-chickens-what-kind-of-education-for-what-kind-of-world/

Access Economics. (2005). *The economic benefit of increased participation in education and training.* The Business Council of Australia and Dusseldorp Skills Forum. Canberra: Access Economics. Retrieved from http://www.bca.com.au/publications/2005-reports-and-papers

Anderson, S. & Kumari, R. (2009). Continuous improvement in schools: Understanding the practice. *International Journal of Educational Development, 29,* 281-292.

Ansess, J., Barnett, E. & Allen, D. (2007). Using research to inform the practice of teachers, schools, and school reform organizations. *Theory into Practice, 46*(4), 325–333.

Aubusson, P., Steele, F., Dinham, S. & Brady, L. (2007). Action learning in teacher learning community formation: Informative or transformative? *Teacher Development, 11*(2), 133- 148.

Australian Curriculum Assessment and Reporting Authority. (2011). *NAPLAN.* Retrieved from http://www.nap.edu.au/naplan/naplan.html

Australian Government. (2009*). Living sustainably: The Australian government's national action plan for education for sustainability.* Environmental Standards Unit: Canberra. Retrieved from www.environment.gov.au/system/files/.../national-action-plan.rtf

Australian Indigenous Education Foundation (2015), *Compendium of Best Practice for achieving successful outcomes with Indigenous students in Australian boarding schools,* Pub. AIEF

Australian Institute for Teaching and School Leadership. (2014a). *Global trends in professional learning and performance & development: Some implications and ideas for the Australian education system.* Retrieved from http://www.aitsl.edu.au/docs/default-source/default-document-library/horizon_scan_report.pdf

Australian Institute for Teaching and School Leadership. (2014b). Global trends in professional learning and performance & development. *Curriculum and Leadership Journal, 12*(9).

Australian Institute for Teaching and School Leadership. (2014b). *Global trends in professional learning and performance & development: Some implications and ideas for the Australian education system.* Retrieved from http://www.aitsl.edu.au/docs/default-source/default-document-library/horizon_scan_report.pdf

Avalos, B. (2011). Teacher professional development in teaching and teacher education over ten years. *Teaching and Teacher Education, 27*(1), 10–20.

Babkie, A. M., & Provost, M. C. (2004). Teachers as Researchers. *Intervention in School and Clinic, 39*(5), 260-268

Bach, J. V., Thul, N. G., & Foord, K. (2004). Tests That Inform. *A Principal Leadership, 4*(6), 39.

Barber, M. & Mourshed, M. (2007). *How the world's best-performing school systems come out on top.* New York: McKinsey and Company.

Barro, R. J. (2001). Human capital and growth. *American Economic Review, 91*(2), 12-17.

Bartlett, S., & Burton, D. (2006). Practitioner research or descriptions of classroom practice? A discussion of teachers investigating their classrooms. *Educational Action Research, 14*(3), 395-405.

Bergan, S., & Damian, R. (Eds.). (2010). Higher education for modern societies. *Council of Europe Higher Education Series, 15.* Retrieved from https://book.coe.int/eur/en/higher-education-and-research/4462-higher-education-for-modern-societies-competences-and-values-council-of-europe-higher-education-series-no15.html

Bissell, J. (2004). Teacher's construction of space and place: The method in the madness. *Forum, 46*(1), 28-32.

Blackmore, J., Bateman, D., Cloonan, A., Dixon, M, Loughlin, J, OMara, J, & Senior, K. (2011). *Innovative learning environments research study.* Retrieved from http://www.learningspaces.edu.au/docs/learningspaces-final-report.pdf

Blank, S. (2011). *Mentors, coaches and teachers.* Retrieved from http://steveblank.com/2011/04/19/mentors-`coaches-and-teachers/

Blau, I. & Presser, O. (2013). e-Leadership of school principals: Increasing school effectiveness. *British Journal of Educational Technology*, *44*(6), 1000–1011.

Bloomfield, D. (2009). Working within and against neoliberal accreditation agendas: Opportunities for professional experience. *Asia-Pacific Journal of Teacher Education*, *37*(1), 27-44.

Board of Studies NSW. (2014). *Educational Resources: NAPLAN.* Retrieved from http://www.boardofstudies.nsw.edu.au/naplan/

Borko, H. (2004). Professional development and teacher learning: Mapping the terrain. *Educational Researcher*, *33*(8), 3-15.

British Educational Communications and Technology Agency. (2008). *ICTs quality indicators.* Retrieved June 10, 2008, from http://feandskills.becta.org.uk/content_files/feandskills/resources/Key_docs/ICTs_quality_indicators_FE.pdf

British Educational Research Association. (2014). *The role of research in teacher education: Reviewing the evidence: Interim report of the BERA-RSA inquiry.* Retrieved from https://www.bera.ac.uk/wp-content/uploads/2014/02/BERA-RSA-Interim-Report.pdf?noredirect=1

Brooks, D. C. (2011). Space matters: The impact of formal learning environments on student learning. *British Journal of Educational Technology*, *42*(5), 719-726.

Brown, M., (2015). *Seven principles for classroom design: The learning space rating system.* Educause Review. Retrieved from http://www.educause.edu/ero/article/seven-principles-classroom-design-learning-space-rating-system

Buckingham, J. (2013). Education policy trends in Australia [online]. *Independence*, *38*(2), 6-7. Retrieved from http://search.informit.com.au.ezproxy.scu.edu.au/documentSummary;dn=173799539531097;res=IELHSS

Buckley, F.,(2000). *Team Teaching: What, How and Why?* Thousand Oaks, CA: Sage Publications inc.

Caldwell, B. (2006). *Re-imagining educational leadership.* Camberwell, Victoria: ACER press.

Chi, M. T. H., & Ohlsson, S. (2005). Complex declarative learning. In K. J. Holyoak & R. G. Morrison (Eds.), *The Cambridge handbook of thinking and reasoning* (pp. 371–399). Cambridge, Massachusetts: Cambridge University Press.

Chinn, C. A., & Brewer, W. F. (1993). The role of anomalous data in knowledge acquisition: A theoretical framework and implications for science instruction. *Review Of Educational Research,63*(1), 1-49. doi:10.2307/1170558

City, E. A. (2013). Leadership in challenging times. *Educational Leadership, 70*(7), 10-14.

City, E., Elmore, R., Fiarman, S. & Teitel, L. (2009). *Instructional rounds in education: A network approach to improving teaching and learning.* Cambridge: Harvard Education Press.

Clutterbuck, D. (1985). *Everyone needs a mentor: How to foster talent within the organization.* London: Institute of Personnel Management.

Cochran-Smith, M. & Donnell, K. (2006). Practitioner inquiry: Blurring the boundaries of research and practice. In G. Camilli, P. Elmore, & J. Green (Eds.) *Complementary Methods for Research in Education* (2nd ed). Washington: AERA.

Coe, R., Aloisi, C., Higgins, S. and Major, L.E., (2014). *What makes great teaching? Review of the underpinning research.* October 2014. Retrieved from http://www.suttontrust.com/wp-content/uploads/2014/10/What-makes-great-teaching-FINAL-4.11.14.pdf

Coggshall, J.G., Rasmussen, C., Colton, A., Milton, J., & Jacques, C. (2012). *Generating teaching effectiveness: The role of job-embedded professional learning in teacher evaluation.* Research & Policy Brief. Retrieved from http://www.gtlcenter.org/sites/default/files/docs/GeneratingTeachingEffectiveness.pdf

Cole, P. (2012). Aligning professional learning, performance management and effective teaching. *Centre for Strategic Education Seminar Series,* Paper no. 217. Retrieved from http://www.ptrconsulting.com.au/sites/default/files/Aligning_professional_learning_performance_management_and_effective_teaching.pdf

Coleman, J., Campbell, E., Hobson, C., McPardand, J., Mood, A., Weinfeld, E., & York, R. (1966). *Equality of educational opportunity.* Washington, DC: Government Printing Office.

Collins, J. (2001). *From Good to Great.* New York: Harper Collins.

Cordingly, P., & Buckler, N. (2012). Mentoring and coaching for teachers continuing professional development. In Fletcher, S., Mullen, C. (Eds.) *SAGE Handbook of Mentoring and Coaching in Education* (pp. 215-227). London: SAGE Publications

Costa, A., & Kallick, B. (1993). Through the lens of a critical friend. *Educational Leadership, 51*(2), 49–51.

Creswell, J. (2002). *Educational research: Planning, conducting and evaluating quantitative and qualitative research.* Upper Saddle Creek, NJ: Pearson Education.

Crowther, F. and Ferguson, M., (2009). *Developing teacher leaders: How teacher leadership enhances school success.* California: Corwin Press

Darling-Hammond, L. (1997). *The right to learn: A blueprint for creating schools that work.* San Francisco: Jossey-Bass.

Darling-Hammond, L. (1997). The right to learn: A blueprint for creating schools that work. *Educational Researcher, 33*(8), 3–15.

Darling-Hammond, L. (2000). Teacher quality and student achievement: A review of state policy evidence. *Education Policy Analysis Archives, 8*(1), 1-50.

Darling-Hammond, L. (2010). Teacher education and the American future. *Journal of Teacher Education, 61*(1-2), 35-47.

Darling-Hammond, L., Amrein-Beardsley, A., Haertel, E. H., & Rothstein, J. (2011). *Getting teacher evaluation right: A background paper for policy makers.* American Educational Research Association and National Academy of Education.

Darling-Hammond, L. & Post, L. (2000). Inequality in teaching and schooling: Supporting high-quality teaching and leadership in low-income schools. In R. D. Kahlenberg (Ed). *A notion at risk: Preserving public education as an engine for social mobility.* New York: The Century Foundation.

Darling-Hammond, L., & Rothman, R. (2011). Lessons learned from Finland, Ontario, and Singapore. In L. Darling-Hammond& R. Rothman (Eds.). *Teacher and leader effectiveness in high-performing education systems* (pp. 1-11). Washington, DC: Alliance for Excellent Education.

Department for Education and Skills (2005). *Mentoring and Coaching CPD capacity building project: National framework for mentoring and coaching.* Retrieved from http://www.curee paccts.com/files/publication/1219925968/National-framework-for-mentoring-and-coaching.pdf

Desimone, L. M., Smith, T. M., & Ueno, K. (2006). Are teachers who need sustained, content-focused professional development getting it? An administrator's dilemma. *Educational Administration Quarterly, 42*(2), 179–215.

DEST. (2001). *Making better connections: Models of teacher professional development for the integration of information and communication technology into classroom practice.* Canberra: Commonwealth Govt Printing Press.

Dickens, L., & Watkins, K. (1999). Action research: Rethinking Lewin. *Management Learning, 30*(2), 127-140

Dijkstra, A. B., & de la Motte, P. I. (Eds.). (2014). *Social Outcomes for Education: The assessment of social outcomes and school improvement through school inspections.* Amsterdam: Amsterdam University Press. Retrieved from http://www.sici-inspectorates.eu/MediaLibrary/sici/Obrazky/ExecutiveCommittee/Publication-SocialOutcomes-of-Education.pdf

Dinham, S. (2008). How to get your school moving and improving: An evidence-based approach. Camberwell, Victoria: Australian Council for Educational.

Doe, T. (2011). *Teacher professional learning partnerships in practice.* Rockhampton, Queensland: CQUniversity.

Doe, T. (2013). *A new way to think about teacher professional learning.* Australia: Primrose Hall Publishing Group.

Doe, T. (2014). An examination of an approach to teacher professional learning. *International Journal of Innovation Creativity and Change, 1*(3). Retrieved from http://www.ijicc.net/index.php/past-editions/14-vol1-issue-3-may-2014.html

Doe, T. (2015). *High impact instructional leadership.* London: Primrose Hall Publishing Group.

Doe, T., ONeill, P., & Lynch, D. (2006). Building Teacher Capability through School/ University Partnerships. *International Journal of Knowledge, Culture and Change Management, 6*(7), 183-190.

Donkin, R. (1998, January 9). Year of the Knowledge Worker. *Financial Times.*

Doyle, L., Kurth, B., & Kerr, E. (2000). *Knowledge work: The rise of the office economy.* Brisbane: National Training Authority Report. Retrieved from http://www.voced.edu.au/content/ngv%3A3959

Driver, R. (1983). *The pupil as scientist?* New York: The McGraw-Hill Companies.

DuFour, R., DuFour, R., Eaker, R., & Many, T. (2010). *Learning by doing: A handbook for professional learning communities at work.* Bloomington, Indiana: Solution Tree Press.

Dufour, R. & Marzano, R. J. (2011). *Leaders of learning: How district, school and classroom leaders improve student achievement.* Bloomington, Indiana: Solution Tree.

Ebmeier, H, & Nicklaus, J. (1999). The impact of peer and principal collaborative supervision on teachers trust commitment, desire for collaboration, and efficacy. *Journal of Curriculum and Supervision, 14*(4), 351-369.

Efron, E., Winter, J. S., & Bressman, S. (2012). Toward a more effective mentoring model: An innovative program of collaboration. *Journal of Jewish Education, 78*, 331–361.

Ellinger, A. D., Ellinger, A. E., & Keller, S. B. (2003). Supervisory coaching behavior, employee satisfaction, and warehouse employee performance: A dyadic perspective in the distribution industry. *Human Resource Development Quarterly, 14*, 435–458.

Elmore, R. (2004). *Reform from the Inside Out.* Cambridge: Harvard University Press.

Elmore, R. (2008). *Usable Knowledge.* Harvard Graduate School of Education. Retrieved from http://www.uknow.gse.harvard.edu/leadership/leadership001a.html

Elmore, R. (2011). *Reciprocal accountability: How effective instructional leaders improve teaching and learning.* Retrieved from https://www.educatornetwork.com/HotTopics/leadershipandinnovation/Reciprocal-Accountability-How-Effective-Instructional-Leaders-Improve-Teaching-and-Learning

Fallon, D. (2006). The buffalo upon the chimneypiece: The value of evidence. *Expanded Academic ASAP, 57*(2), 139+. Retrieved from http://go.galegroup.com/ps/i.do?id=GALE%7CA143062816&v=2.1&u=scu_au&it=r&p=EAIM&sw=w&asid=9ba294869af3bc273989928486f67864

Ferrandino, V. L. (2014). Challenges for 21st-century elementary school principals. *Phi Delta Kappan, 82*(6), 440.

Fishman, B., Marx, R., Best, S., & Tal, R. (2003). Linking teacher and student learning to improve professional development in systemic reform. *Teaching and Teacher Education, 19*(6), 643-658.

Fogarty, W. (2012). *Learning for the western world? The Indigenous education dilemma.* Retrieved from http://theconversation.com/learning-for-the-western-world-the-indigenous-education-dilemma-11326

Fowler, M. (2012). Leading inquiry at a teacher level: It's all about mentorship. *Set: Research Information for Teachers*, *3*, 2-7. Retrieved from http://search.informit.com.au.ezproxy.scu.edu.au/documentS ummary;dn=058864112219530;res=IELHSS

Freebody, P. (2003). *Qualitative Research in Education*. London: Sage Publishers.

Fullan, M. (2006). *Quality leadership ⇔ quality learning: Proof beyond reasonable doubt*. Chapter prepared for the Irish Primary Principals Network. Cork, Ireland: Líonra+.

Fullan, M. (2006). *Turnaround leadership*. San Francisco: Jossey-Bass.

Fullan, M. (2007). *The new meaning of educational change.* New York: Teachers College Press.

Fullan, M. (2008). *The Six Secrets of Change: What the Best Leaders do to help their organisations survive and thrive.* Jossey-Bass, San Francisco.

Fullan, M. (2011). *Choosing the wrong drivers for whole system reform.* Summary of Seminar Series Paper No. 204. Retrieved from http://edsource.org/wp-content/uploads/Fullan-Wrong-Drivers1.pdf

Fullan, M. (2011). *Learning is the work*. Unpublished paper. Retrieved from http://www.michaelfullan.ca/media/13396087260.pdf

Garet, M., Porter, A., Desimone, L., Birman, B., & Yoon, K. (2001). What makes professional development effective? Results from a national sample or teachers. *American Educational Research Journal*, *38*(4), 915.

Gilley, J. W., Morris, M. L., Waite, A. M., Coates, T., & Veliquette, A. (2010). Integrated theoretical model for building effective teams. *Advances In Developing Human Resources*, *12*(1), 7-28. doi:10.1177/1523422310365309

Glazer, E. M. & Hannafin, M. J. (2006). The collaborative apprenticeship model: Situated professional development within school settings. *Teaching & Teacher Education: An International Journal Of Research And Studies*, *22*(2), 179- 193.

Gong, R., Chen, S. Y., & Yang, M. L. (2014). Career outcome of employees: The mediating effect of mentoring. *Social Behavior & Personality: an international journal*, *42*(3), 487-501.

Griffin, P. Care, E. & McGraw, B. (2012). The Changing Role of Education and Schools. In P. Griffin, E. Care, & B. McGraw

(Eds.), *Assessment and teaching of 21st Century Skills* (pp. 1-15). Netherlands: Springer.

Gronn, P. (2000). Distributed properties: A new architecture for leadership. *Educational Management and Administration, 28*(3), 317-338.

Haertel, G., Means, B. & Penuel, W. (2007). Technology tools for collecting, managing, and using assessment data to inform instruction and improve achievement. *Yearbook Of The National Society For The Study Of Education (Wiley-Blackwell), 106*(2), 103-132. doi:10.1111/j.1744-7984.2007.00117.x

Hamel, G. & Zanini, M. (2014). *Build a change platform, not a change program.* Retrieved from http://www.mckinsey.com/insights/organization/build_a_change_ platform_not_a_change_program

Hamilton, L., Halverson, R., Jackson, S., Mandinach, E., Supovitz, J., & Wayman, J. (2009). *Using student achievement data to support instructional decision making.* Washington, DC: National Center for Education Evaluation and Regional Assistance, Institute of Education Sciences, U.S. Department of Education.

Hamlin, R. G., Ellinger, A. E., & Beattie, R. S. (2008). The emergent coaching industry: A wake-up call for HRD professionals. *Human Resource Development International, 11*, 287-305.

Hanushek, E. & Woessmann, L. (2010). *The high cost of low educational performance: The long-run economic impact of improving PISA outcomes.* Paris: OECD Publishing.

Hanushek, E. A. & Ludger W. (2009). *Do better schools lead to more growth? Cognitive skills, economic outcomes, and causation.* Retrieved from http://www.nber.org/papers/w14633.pdf

Hardwell, S., (2003). *Teacher Professional Development: It's not an event: it's a process.* Texas, USA: CORD

Hargreaves, A. (2007). Five flaws of staff developments and the future beyond. *Journal of Staff Development, 28*(3), 37–38

Hargreaves, A. & Fullan, M. (2012). *Professional capital: Transforming teaching in every school.* New York: Teachers College Press.

Hattie, J. (1999) *Influences on student learning.* Retrieved from http://www.education.auckland.ac.nz/webdav/site/education/share d/hattie/docs/influences-on-student-learning.pdf

Hattie, J. (2003). Teachers make a difference: What is the research evidence?. *Proceedings of Australian Council for Educational Research Annual Conference, Melbourne, 19–21 October.*

Retrieved from
http://research.acer.edu.au/research_conference_2003/4

Hattie, J (2005). What is the nature of evidence that makes a difference to learning? Paper presented at the Australian Council for Educational Research Conference. *Using Data to Support Learning, Melbourne, 7-9 August*. Retrieved from www.acer.edu.au/workshops/documents/Hattie.pdf

Hattie, J. (2009). *Visible learning: A synthesis of over 800 meta-analyses relating to achievement*. Abingdon: Routledge.

Hattie, J. (2011). *Challenge of Focusing Education Reform*. Retrieved from http://www.theaustralian.com.au/business/news/rethinking-education-the-challenge-of-focusing-reform/story-fn8ex0p1-1226069556190

Hattie, J. (2012). Know thy impact. *Educational Leadership, 70*(1), 18-23.

Hattie, J. (2012). *Visible Learning for Teachers: maximizing Impact On Learning*. London and New York: Routledge.

Hattie, J. & Timperley, H. (2007). The power of feedback. *Review of Educational Research, 77*(1), 81-112.

Helmer, J., Bartlett, C., Wolgemuth, J. R. & Lea, T. (2011). Coaching (and) commitment: Linking ongoing professional development, quality teaching and student outcomes. *Professional Development in Education, 37*(2), 197-211.

Hennessey S., & Deaney, R. (2004). *Sustainability and evolution of ICTs-supported classroom*. Oxford: Practice University of Cambridge, Faculty of Education.

Hennessey S., & Deaney, R. (2007). Sustainability, evolution and the dissemination of information communication technology-supported classroom practice. *Research Papers in Education, 22*(1), 65-94.

Hiebert, J., Gallimore, R., & Stigler, J. W. (2002). A knowledge base for the teaching profession: What would it look like and how can we get one? *Educational Researcher, 31*(5), 3–15.

Hipp, K. K., Huffman, J. B., Pankake, A. M., & Olivier, D. F. (2008). Sustaining professional learning Communities: Case studies. *Journal of Educational Change, 9*, 173-195.

Hirt, M. & Willmott, P. (2014). Strategic principles for competing in the digital age. *McKinsey Quarterly*. Retrieved from http://www.mckinsey.com/insights/strategy/strategic_principles_for_competing_in_the_digital_age

Hogan, J. (2001). *Action Learning, QTP Project, WACA referenced in ANSN QTP Action Learning Kit The Reflective Teacher*. Perth, WA: DETWA.

Hopkins, D. (2008). *A teacher's guide to classroom research*. Maidenhead, United Kingdom: Open University Press.

Hutchinson, S., & Purcell, J. (2007). *Learning and the line: The role of line managers in training, learning and development*. London, UK: CIPD.

Ikemoto, G., & Marsh, J. (2007). Cutting through the data-driven mantra: Different conceptions of data-driven decision making. *Yearbook of the National Society for the Study of Education, 106*(1), 105-131.

Ingvarson, L., Beavis, A., & Kleinhenz, E. (2005). Factors affecting the impact of teacher education courses on teacher preparedness. *Annual Meeting of the American Educational Research Association, Montreal, April 11-15.*

Jamieson, P., Fisher, K., Gilding, T., Taylor, P. G., & Trevitt, A. C. F. (2000). Place and space in the design of new learning environments. *Higher Education Research and Development, 19*(2), 221-236.

Jensen, B. (2011). *Better teacher appraisal and feedback: Improving performance*. Retrieved from http://grattan.edu.au/static/files/assets/a9daf733/081_report_teacher_appraisal.pdf

Joo, B., Sushko, J. S., & McLean, G. N. (2012). Multiple faces of coaching: Manager-as-coach, executive coaching, and formal mentoring. *Organization Development Journal, 30*, 19-38.

Kane, T. (2013). *Measures of effective teaching project releases final research report*. Retrieved from http://www.gatesfoundation.org/media-center/press-releases/2013/01/measures-of-effective-teaching-project-releases-final-research-report

Katzenmeyer, M., & Moller, G. (2001). *Awakening the sleeping giant: Leadership development for teachers*. Thousand Oaks, California: Corwin Press.

Kennedy, M. (1998). *Form and substance in in-service teacher education (Research monograph no. 13)*. Arlington, Virginia: National Science Foundation.

Kim, S., Egan, T. M., Kim, W., & Kim, J. (2013). The impact of managerial coaching behavior on employee work-related reactions. *Journal of Business and Psychology*, *28*, 315–330.

Kirschner, P. A., Sweller, J., Clark, R. E. (2006) Why minimal guidance during instruction does not work: An analysis of the failure of constructivist, discovery, problem-based, experiential, and inquiry-based teaching. *Educational Psychologist*, *41*(2), 75–86.

Kozloff, M. A. (2005). Fads in general education: Fad, fraud, and folly. In J. W. Jacobson, R. M. Foxx, J. A. Mulick, J. W. Jacobson, R. M. Foxx, & J. A. Mulick (Eds.). *Controversial therapies for developmental disabilities: Fad, fashion and science in professional practice* (pp. 159-173). Mahwah, NJ, US: Lawrence Erlbaum Associates Publishers.

Kram, K. E. (1985). *Mentoring at work: Developmental relationships in organizational life*. Glenview, Illinois: Scott, Foresman.

Kram, K. E. & Isabella, L. (1985). Mentoring alternatives: The role of peer relationships in career development. *Academy of Management Journal, 28*(1), 110-132.

Kroth, M., & Keeler, C. (2009). Caring as a Managerial Strategy. *Human Resource Development Review*, *8*(4), 506-531.

Lackney, J, & Jacobs, P. (2002). *Teachers as placemakers: Investigating teachers use of the physical learning environment in instructional design*. US Department of Education.

Lawless, K. A., & Pellegrino, J. W. (2007). Professional development in integrating technology into teaching and learning: Knowns, unknowns, and ways to pursue better questions and answers. *Review of Educational Research*, *77*(4) 575-614.

Lagemann, E. C. (1996). *Contested terrain: A history of education research in the United States, 1890–1990*. Chicago: Spencer Foundation.

Lee, V. E., & Smith, J. B. (1996). Collective responsibility for learning and its effects on gains in achievement for early secondary school students. *American Journal of Education, 104*, 103-147.

Leithwood, K. A., Harris, A., & Hopkins, D. (2008). Seven strong claims about successful school leadership. *School Leadership and Management*, *28*(1), 27-42.

Leithwood, K., & Jantzi, D. (2000a). The effects of transformational leadership on organisational conditions and student engagement. *Journal of Educational Administration, 38*(2), 112-129.

Leithwood, K., & Jantzi, D. (2000b). Principal and teacher leadership effects: A replication. *School Leadership & Management, 20*(4), 415-434.

Leithwood, K., Seashore L. K., Anderson, S., & Wahlstrom, K. (2004), *How leadership Influences Student Learning.* New York: Wallace Foundation.

Levine, T. H., & Marcus, A. S. (2010). How the structure and focus of teachers collaborative activities facilitate and constrain teacher learning. *Teaching and Teacher Education, 26*(3), 389-398.

Lewis, A. C. (2002). Washington commentary: School reform and professional development. *Phi Delta Kappan, 83*(7).

Lippincott, J. K. (2009). Learning spaces: Involving faculty to improve pedagogy. *Educause Review, 44*(2), 16-18.

Little, J. W. (2003). Inside teacher community: Representations of classroom practice. *Teachers College Record, 105*(6), 913–45.

Louis, K. S., & Marks, H. M. (1998). Does professional community affect the classroom? Teachers work and student experiences in restructuring schools. *American Journal of Education, 106*, 532-575.

Louis, K.S., Leithwood, K., Wahlstrom, K., & Anderson, S. (2010). *Investigating the links to improved student learning: Final report of research findings.* New York: The Wallace Foundation. Retrieved from www.wallacefoundation.org/knowledge-center/school-leadership/key-research/Pages/Investigating-the-Links-to-Improved-Student-Learning.aspx.

Lu, H. L. (2010). Research on peer coaching in preservice teacher education – A review of literature. *Teaching and Teacher Education, 26*(4), 748–753.

Lynch, D. (2004). *A comparison of the Bachelor of Learning Management and the Bachelor of Education in the context of a knowledge economy.* Doctoral Thesis. Rockhampton: Central Queensland University.

Lynch, D. (2012). *Preparing teachers in times of change: Teaching school, standards, new content and evidence.* Brisbane: Primrose Hall.

Lynch, D. and Madden, J. (2014) Enabling Teachers to Better Teach Through Engaging with Research. *International Journal for Cross-Disciplinary Subjects in Education.* (In publication process)

Lynch, D., & Smith, R. (2006). The learning management design process. In D. Lynch & R. Smith (Eds.). *The rise of the learning manager* (pp. 53-67). Frenchs Forest, NSW: Pearson Education Australia.

Lynch, D. & Smith, R. (2007). Australian schooling: What future?. In R. Smith, D. Lynch & B. A. Knight (Eds.), *Learning management: Transitioning teachers for national and international change.* Frenchs Forest, NSW: Pearson Education Australia.

Lynch, D. & Smith, R. (2011). *Designing the Classroom Curriculum in the Knowledge Age.* Sydney: AACLM Press.

Lynch, D. & Smith, R. (2012). *Assessing and Reporting the Classroom Curriculum in the Knowledge Age.* London: Primrose Hall.

Lynch, D. & Smith, R. (2013). The challenge of changing teacher education. In D. Lynch & T. Yeigh (Eds.), *Teacher education in Australia: Investigations into programming, practicum and partnership* (pp 27-40). Brisbane: Oxford Global Press.

Lynch, D., Smith, R., & Doe, T. (2007). The design and execution of learning experiences: the Learning Management Plan. In R. Smith, D. Lynch, & B. Knight (Eds.), *Learning management: transitioning teachers for national and international change* (pp. 75-105). Frenchs Forest, NSW: Pearson Education Australia.

MacBeath, J., & Dempster, N. (2009). *Connecting leadership and learning.* New York, NY: Routledge.

McCormick, R. (2010). The state of the nation in CPD: A literature review. *The Curriculum Journal, 21*(4), 395–412.

McWilliam, E. & Haukka, S. (2008). Educating the creative workforce: New directions for twenty-first century schooling. *British Educational Research Journal, 34*(5) 651–666.

Madden, J. (2012), School improvement: Innovation for the future. In R. Smith & D. Lynch, *Case studies in education: Leadership and innovation* (pp. 148-174). Brisbane: Primrose Hall Publishing Group.

Madden, J. (2012). *The school improvement challenge: How the principal can harness teacher leadership to improve student learning.* Brisbane: Primrose Hall Press.

Madden, J. (2013). The learner of today needs a teacher focused on tomorrow. In J. Madden & R. Smith (Eds.), *Teachers talk about whats important: Selected papers from the 2012 teacher education dialogue conference* (pp. 14-24). Brisbane, Qld: Primrose Hall Publishing Group.

Madden, J. & Lynch, D. (2014). Enabling teachers to better teach through engaging with research. *International Journal for Cross-Disciplinary Subjects in Education,* 4(1), 1790-1797.

Madden, J., Wilks, J., Maoine, M., Loader, N., & Robinson, N. (2012). Journeying together: Understanding the process of teacher change and the impacts on student learning. *International studies in educational administration, 40*(2), 19-36.

Mangiante, E. M. S. (2011). Teachers matter: Measures of teacher effectiveness in low-income minority schools. *Educational Assessment, Evaluation and Accountability, 23*(1), 41-63

Mavrinac, M. A. (2005). Transformational leadership: Peer mentoring as a values-based learning process. *Libraries and the Academy, 5*(3), 391–404.

Marzano, R. (2003). *What Works in Schools: Translating Research into Action,* ASCD

Marzano, R. J. (2007). *The art and science of teaching.* Virginia: ASCD.

Marzano, R. J. (2012). *Marzano school leadership evaluation model.* Marzano Research Laboratory. Retrieved from http://www.marzanocenter.com/Leadership-Evaluation/

Marzano, R., & Pickering, D. (2006). *Dimensions of learning teacher's manual.* Aurora, Colorado: Mid-continent Regional Education Laboratory.

Marzano, R. J., Pickering, D. J., Arredondo, D. E., Blackburn, G. J., Brandt, R. S., Moffett, C. A., … Whisler, J. S. (1997). *Dimensions of learning teacher's manual.* (2nd ed.). Aurora, Colorado: Mid-continent Regional Educational Laboratory.

Marzano, R. J., Pickering, D. J., & Pollock, J. E. (2001). *Classroom instruction that works: Research-based strategies for increasing student achievement.* Alexandria, Virginia: ASCD.

Marzano, R., Waters, T., & McNulty, B. (2005). *School Leadership that Works.* Alexandria, VA: Association for Supervision and Curriculum Development.

Maughan, S., Teeman, D. & Wilson, R. (2012). *What leads to positive change in teaching practice.* NFER Research Programme: Developing the Education Workforce. Slough: NFER.

Menter, I. (2011). Four academic sub-tribes, but one territory? Teacher educators and teacher education in Scotland. *Journal of Education for Teaching: International research and pedagogy, 37*(3), 293-308.

Mendels, P. (2012) The effective principal. *JSD, 33*(1), 54-58. Retrieved from http://www.wallacefoundation.org/knowledge-center/school-leadership/effective-principal-leadership/documents/the-effective-principal.pdf

Mid-continent Research for Education and Learning. (2000). *Asking the right questions: A leaders guide to systems thinking about school improvement.* Aurora, Colorado: US Department of Education.

Mills, G. (2000). *Action research: A guide for the teacher researcher.* Upper Saddle River, New Jersey: Pearson, Allyn & Bacon.

Miller R. J., & Rowan, B. *(2006)*. Effects of organic management on student achievement. *American Educational Research Journal, 43*(2), 219–253.

Miller, G. (2012) *Understanding John Hattie's visible learning research in the context of Carol Dweck's growth mindset.* Retrieved from https://www.google.com.au/webhp?tab=mw&ei=02HhU_etOeeps QSgm4CIDQ&ved=0CAUQqS4oAg#q=Understanding+John+Ha ttie%E2%80%99s+Visible+Learning+Research+in+the+Context+ of+Carol+Dweck% 2%80%99s+Growth+Mindset.

Ministerial Advisory Committee For Educational Renewal. (2004). *Professional development for teachers in an era of innovation.* Retrieved from http://www.smartstate.qld.gov.au/resources/publications/index.shtm

Ministerial Council on Education, Employment, Training & Youth Affairs. (2008). *Melbourne declaration on educational goals for young Australians.* Retrieved from http://www.curriculum.edu.au/verve/_resources/National_Declara tion_on_the_Educational_Goals_for_Young_Australians.pdf

Mourshed, M., Chijioke, C., Barber, M. (2010). *How the worlds most improved school systems keep getting better.* Retrieved from http://www.mckinsey.com/client_service/social_sector/latest_thin king/worlds_most_improved_schools.

Mulford, B. (2008) *The leadership challenge: Improving learning in schools.* Retrieved from http://research.acer.edu.au/cgi/viewcontent.cgi?article=1000&cont ext=aer

National Institute for Urban School Improvement (2000), *Improving education: the promise of Inclusive Schooling,* <http://www.ldonline.org/article/209> viewed 11 July 2015

Nisbet, S. (2005). Using assessment data to inform planning and teaching: The case of state-wide benchmark numeracy tests. In B. J. Bartlett, F. Bryer, & D. Roebuck (Eds.), *Stimulating the "action" as participants in participatory research* (pp. 26-38). Nathan, Queensland: Griffith University, School of Cognition, Langauge and Special Education.

Nowotny, H., Scott, P., & Gibbons, M. (2002). *Rethinking science: Knowledge and the public in an age of uncertainty.* London: Polity.

Nuthall, G. (2004). Relating classroom teaching to student learning: A critical analysis. *Harvard Educational Review, 74*(3), 273-306.

Opfer, V. & Pedder, D. (2011). Conceptualizing teacher professional learning. *Review of Educational Research,* 81(3), 376–407.

Organization for Economic Co-operation and Development. (2001). *The wellbeing of nations: The role of human and social capital.* Paris: Author.

Organisation for Economic Co-operation and Development. (2009). *Creating effective teaching and learning environments: First results from TALIS.* Paris: OECD Publishing. Retrieved from http://www.oecd.org/edu/school/43023606.pdf

Organisation for Economic Co-operation and Development. (2010a). *The high costs of low performance.* Paris: OECD Publishing.

Organisation for Economic Co-operation and Development. (2010b). *Strong performers and successful reformers in education lessons from PISA for the United States.* Paris: OECD Publishing.

Organisation for Economic Co-operation and Development. (2011). Education and skills. In OECD (Ed.) *How's Life? Measuring Well-being (pp. 145-168).* Paris: OECD Publishing. DOI: http://dx.doi.org/10.1787/9789264121164-9-en

Organisation for Economic Co-operation and Development. (2013). *Leadership for the 21ˢᵗ century learning, educational research and innovation.* Paris: OECD Publishing. Retrieved from http://dx.doi.org/10.1787/9789264205406-en

Organisation for Economic Co-operation and Development. (2013). *Upgrading skills for current and future needs, in perspectives on global development 2013: industrial policies in a changing world.* Paris: OECD Publishing. Retrieved from http:dx.doi.org/10.1787/persp_glob_dev-2013-10-en

Organisation for Economic Co-operation and Development. (1996). *The knowledge-based economy.* Paris: OECD Publishing.

Oser, F. K., & Baeriswyl, F. J. (2001). Choreographies of teaching: Bridging instruction to learning. In V. Richardson (Ed.),

Handbook of research on teaching, (pp. 1031–1065). Washington, DC: American educational research association.

Tee Ng, P. (2012). Mentoring and coaching educators in the Singapore education system. *International Journal of Mentoring and Coaching in Education*, *3*(1), 24-35.

Paustian-Underdahl, S. C., Shanock, L. R., Rogelberg, S. G., Scott, C. W., Justice, L., & Altman, D. G. (2013). Antecedents to supportive supervision: An examination of biographical data. *Journal of Occupational and Organizational Psychology*, *86*, 288–309.

Pearson Foundation. (2013). *Strong performers and successful reformers in education*. Retrieved from http://www.pearsonfoundation.org/oecd/germany.html#sthash.kJr E42hZ.dpuf

Pfeffer, J. (1994). *Competitive advantage through people: Unleashing the power of the work force*. Boston: Harvard Business School Press.

Popper, K. (1972). *Objective knowledge*. London: Oxford University Press.

Portner, H. (2008). *Mentoring new teachers*. Thousand Oaks, CA: Corwin.

Powell, D. R., & Diamond, K. E. (2011). Improving the outcomes of coaching-based professional development interventions. In S. B. Neuman & D. K. Dickinson (Eds.), *Handbook of early literacy research* (pp. 295–307). New York: Guilford.

Powell, W. W. & Snellman, K. (2004). The knowledge economy. *Annual Review of Sociology*, *30*, 199–220. Retrieved from http://scholar.harvard.edu/files/kaisa/files/powell_snellman.pdf

Purser, S. R., Knight, H. V., & Bedenbaugh, E. H. (1990). *The relationship between secondary principal's evaluation of teachers and pupil achievement*. Chapter presented at the annual meeting of the American Educational Research Association, Boston.

Putnam, R. T. & Borko, H. (2000). What do new views of knowledge and thinking have to say about research on teacher learning? *Educational Researcher*, *29*(1), 4-15.

Reason, P., & Bradbury, H. (2006). *Handbook of action research*. Retrieved from http://faculty.mu.edu.sa/public/uploads/1346012794.621handbook _of_action_research.pdf

Rhodes, D.,& Spiers, H., (2013), Creating Educational Equity for Indigenous Students through Significant Organisational Change. *The International Journal of Educational Organisation and Leadership*, 19(4), 27-37.

Rhodes, D.,& Spiers, H., (2013), Creating sustainable Indigenous student leadership in a multicultural learning community in Northern Australia. *Teachers Talk about what's important: Selected papers from the 2012 International Teacher Education Dialogue Conference*, 71-79, Queensland, Australia.

Rhodes, D.,& Spiers, H., (2014), Equipping teachers to empower Indigenous students to be capable leaders across cultures and generations, Paper presented at DPR conference Feb 2014 www.dprconference.com

Roberts, K., & Owens, S. (2012). *Innovative education: A review of the literature*. Adelaide: DECD.

Robinson, K. (2010). *RSA - Changing Education Paradigms*. Retrieved from http://www.youtube.com/watch?v=zDZFcDGpL4U

Robinson, V., Hohepa, M., & Lloyd, C. (2009). *School leadership and student outcomes: Identifying what works and why. Best Evidence Synthesis Iteration (BES).* Wellington: Ministry of Education.

Rodwell, M. & Sale, C. (2011). Using assessment information to inform evidence-based teaching. [online]. *Practically Primary, 16*(1), 37-39. Retrieved from http://search.informit.com.au.ezproxy.scu.edu.au/fullText;dn=185 962;res=AEIPT

Ronfeldt, M., Farmer, S.O., & McQueen, K. (2015). Teacher Collaboration in Instructional Teams and Student Achievement. *American Educational Research Journal*. June 2015 52: 475-514,

Roseler, K. & Dentzau, M. (2013). Teacher professional development: A different perspective. *Cultural Studies of Science Education, 8,* 619-622.

Ross, D., Adams, A., Bondy, E., Dana, N., Dodman, S., & Swain, C. (2011). Preparing teacher leaders: Perceptions of the impact of a cohort-based, job embedded, blended teacher leadership program. *Teaching and Teacher Education, 27*(8), 1213-1222.

Sachs, J., & Parsell, M. (Eds.) (2014). *Peer review of learning and teaching in higher education.* New York: Springer.

St-Jean, E., & Audet, J. (2013). The effect of mentor intervention style in novice entrepreneur mentoring relationships. *Mentoring & Tutoring: Partnership in Learning, 21*(1), 96-119.

Sasson, D.B. & Somech, A., (2014). Observing Aggression of Teachers in School Teams. Teachers and Teaching: Theory and Practice. Retrieved form http://dx.dot.org/10.1080/13540602.2015.1005865

Saunders, W., Goldenberg, C., & Gallimore, R. (2009). Increasing achievement by focusing grade-level teams on improving classroom learning: A prospective, quasi-experimental study of Title I schools. *American Educational Research Journal, 46*(4), 1006–1033.

Scheerens, J., (2013). *What is effective schooling? A review of current thought and practice.* Retrieved from http://www.ibo.org/globalassets/publications/ib-research/whatiseffectiveschoolingfinal-1.pdf

Schiemann, W. A. (2009b). *Reinventing talent management: How to maximize performance in the new marketplace.* Hoboken, New Jersey: John Wiley & Sons.

Schiemann, W. A. (2012). *The ACE advantage: How smart companies unleash talent for optimal performance.* Alexandria, Virginia: Society for Human Resource Management.

Schiemann, W. A., Seibert, J. H., & Morgan, B. S. (2013). *Hidden drivers of success: Leveraging employee insights for strategic advantage.* Alexandria, Virginia: Society for Human Resource Management.

Schiemann, W. A. (2014). From talent management to talent optimization. *Journal of World Business, 49,* 281-288.

Schildkamp, K. & Kuiper, W. (2010). Data-informed curriculum reform: Which data, what purposes, and promoting and hindering factors. *Teaching and Teacher Education, 26*(3), 482–496.

Schleicher, A. (Ed.). (2012). *Preparing teachers and developing school leaders for the 21st Century: Lessons from around the World.* OECD Publishing. Retrieved from www.oecd.org/site/eduistp2012/49850576.pdf

Sebastian, J. & Allensworth, E. (2012). The influence of principal leadership on classroom instruction and student learning: A study of mediated pathways to learning. *Educational Administration Quarterly, 48*(4), 626- 663.

Seibert, J. H. & Schiemann, W. A. (2010). Power to the people. *Quality Progress, 43*(4), 24-30.

Silins, H., Zarins, S., & Mulford, B. (2002). What characteristics and processes define a school as a learning organisation? Is this a useful concept to apply to schools?. *International Education Journal, 3*(1), 24-32. Retrieved from http://ehlt.flinders.edu.au/education/iej/articles/v3n1/silins/paper.pdf

Slavin, R. E. (1997) *Sand, bricks, and seeds: School change strategies and readiness for reform.* Retrieved from http://www.successforall.org/SuccessForAll/media/PDFs/Sand-Bricks---Seedswabstrac.pdf

Smith, R. (2000). The future of teacher education: principles and prospects. *Asia-Pacific Journal of Teacher Education, 28*(1), 7-28.

Smith, T. M., & Ingersoll, R. M. (2004). What Are the Effects of Induction and Mentoring on Beginning Teacher Turnover?. *American Educational Research Journal, 41*(3), 681-714.

Smith, R. & Lynch, D. (2006). *The rise of the learning manager: Changing teacher education.* Frenchs Forest, NSW: Pearson Education Australia.

Smith, R., & Lynch, D. (2010). *Rethinking teacher education: Teacher education in a knowledge age.* Sydney: AACLM Press.

Sogunro, O. A. (2012). Stress in school administration: Coping tips for principals. *Journal of School Leadership* 22(3), 664.

Spaten, O. M. & Flensborg, W. (2013). When middle managers are doing employee coaching. *International Coaching Psychology Review, 8*(2), 18-39.

Stanulis, R. N., & Floden, R. E. (2009). Intensive mentoring as a way to help beginning teachers develop a balanced instruction. *Journal of Teacher Education, 60*(2), 112–122.

Stephenson, J. (1999). *Corporate capability: Implications for the style and direction of work-based learning.* Public lecture given at the University of Technology, Sydney. Retrieved from http://pandora.nla.gov.au/pan/22468/20021106/www.uts.edu.au/fac/edu/rcvet/working%20chapters/9914Stephenson.pdf

Stoll, L., Bolam, R., McMahon, A., Thomas, S., Wallace, M., Greenwood, A., & Hawkey, K. (2006). *Professional learning communites: Source materials for school leaders and other leaders of professional learning.* London: Innovation Unit, DfES, NCSL and GTC.

Stringer, E. (1999). *Action Research in Education.* Thousand Oaks, California: Sage Publications.

Stronge, J. H., Ward, T. J., & Grant, L. W. (2011). What makes good teachers good? A cross-case analysis of the connection between teacher effectiveness and student achievement. *Journal of Teacher Education, 62*(4), 339-355.

Susing, I., & Cavanagh, M. J. (2013). At the intersection of performance: Personality and adult development in coaching. *International Coaching Psychology Review, 8*, 258-69.

Swaffield, S. & Dempster, N. (2009). A learning dialogue. In J. MacBeath, & N. Dempster (Eds.), *Connecting leadership and learning* (pp. 106–120). New York: Routledge.

Taylor, M, Yates, A. Meyer, L & Kinsella, P. (2011). Teacher professional leadership in support of teacher professional development. *Teaching and Teacher Education, 12*(1), 85–94.

Theeboom, T., Beersma, B., & van Vianen, A. E. M. (2014). Does coaching work? A meta-analysis on the effects of coaching on individual level outcomes in an organizational context. *Journal of Positive Psychology. 9*(1), 1-18.

Thompson, G. & Cook, I. (2014). Education policy-making and time. *Journal of Education Policy, 29*(5), 700-715.

Tillema, H. H. (2000). Belief change towards self-directed learning in student teachers: immersion in practice or reflection on action. *Teaching and Teacher Education* 16, 575-591.

Timperley, H. S. (2005). Instructional leadership challenges: The case of using student achievement information for instructional improvement. *Leadership and Policy in Schools, 4*, 3-22.

Timperley, H., Wilson, R., Barrar, H., & Fung, I. (2009). *Teacher professional learning and development.* Wellington: Ministry of Education.

Tolley, H. & Shulruf, B. (2009). From data to knowledge: The interaction between data management systems in educational institutions and the delivery of quality education. *Computers & Education, 53*(4), 1199–1206.

Tomlinson, C. A. (1999). *The differentiated classroom: Responding to the needs of all learners.* Virginia: ASCD.

Tomlinson, P. (2008) Psychological theory and pedagogical effectiveness: The learning promotion potential framework. *British Journal of Educational Psychology, 78*, 507–526.

Tomlinson, C. A., & Allan, S. D. (2000). *Leadership for differentiating schools and classrooms.* Alexandria, Virginia: Association for Supervision and Curriculum Development.

Tomlinson, C. A., Brighton, C., Hertberg, H., Callahan, C., Moon, T., Brimijoin, K, . . . Reynods, T. (2003). Differentiating instruction in response to student readiness, interest and learning profile in academically diverse classrooms: A review of the literature. *Journal for the Education of the Gifted, 27*, 199-245.

Treadwell, M. (2011). *Whatever were we thinking: How the brain learns.* Retrieved from http://www.marktreadwell.com

United Arab Emirates (2014, October 13). Retrieved from http://www.nationsencyclopedia.com/economies/Asia-and-the-Pacific/United-Arab-Emirates.html, viewed 9 July 2015

Valente, T. W. (2005). Network models and methods for studying the diffusion of innovations. In P.J. Carrington, J. Scott, & S. Wasserman (Eds.) *Models and methods in social network analysis* (pp. 98–116). Cambridge: Cambridge University Press.

Vescio, V., Ross, D., & Adams, A. (2008). A review of research on the impact of professional learning communities on teaching practice and student learning. *Teaching and Teacher Education, 24*(1), 80-91.

Walker, J. D., Brooks, D. C., & Baepler, P. (2011). Pedagogy and space: Empirical research on new learning environments. *Educause Quarterly, 34*(4), 4.

The Wallace Foundation (2012). The *school principal as leader: Guiding schools to better teaching and learning.* New York: Author.

Waters, T., Marzano, R. J., & McNulty, B. (2003) *Balanced leadership: What 30 years of research tells us about the effect of leadership on student achievement.* Retrieved from http://www.ctc.ca.gov/educator-prep/ASC/5031RR_BalancedLeadership.pdf

Wiggins, G. (2012). Seven keys to effective feedback. *Educational Leadership, 70*(1), 11–16.

Wikoff, D. (2013). Life Cycle Engineering. Retrieved from http://www.reliableplant.com/Read/23535/communicate-effectively-change-process

Wiliam, D. (2007/2008). Changing classroom practice. *Educational Leadership, 65*(4), 36–42.

Wilson, B 2014, *A Share in the Future: Review of Indigenous Education in the Northern Territory*, Northern Territory Government.

Yang, L., Xu, X., Allen, T., Shi, K., Zhang, X., & Lou, Z. (2011). Mentoring in China: Enhanced understanding and association with occupational stress. *Journal of Business & Psychology, 26*(4), 485-499.

Young, V. M., & Kim, D. H. (2010). Using assessments for instructional improvement: A literature review. *Education Policy Analysis Archives, 18*(19). Retrieved from http://epaa.asu.edu/ojs/article/view/809

Zachay, L. J. (2005). *Creating a mentoring culture: The organizations guide.* New York: Jossey-Bass.

Zeichner, K. (2010). Rethinking the connections between campus courses and field experiences in college-and university-based teacher education. *Journal of Teacher Education, 61*(1-2), 89-99.

137129